SCRIPTURE DAY BY DAY

Bart Tesoriero

Nihil Obstat: Right Reverend Archimandrite Francis Vivona,
                  S.T.M., J.C.L.

Imprimatur: Most Reverend Joseph A. Pepe, D.D., J.C.D.

Date: February 29, 2016

ISBN 978-1-61796-174-8
Library of Congress Number: 2015948938

Artwork © 2016 Michael Adams • Licensee Aquinas Press
Text © 2016 Aquinas Press, Phoenix, Arizona
Printed in China

Table of Contents

Opening and Closing Prayers

Come Holy Spirit

Come, Holy Spirit, fill the hearts of Your faithful, and enkindle in us the fire of Your divine Love. Send forth Your Spirit and we shall be created, and You shall renew the face of the earth. **Let us pray:** O God, who by the light of Your Holy Spirit, has instructed the hearts of Your faithful, grant us by the same Spirit to be truly wise and ever to rejoice in His consolation, through the same Christ our Lord. Amen.

Prayer after Reading the Holy Scriptures
-Saint Bede the Venerable

Let me not, O Lord, be puffed up with worldly wisdom, which passes away, but grant me that love which never abates, that I may not choose to know anything among men but Jesus, and Him crucified.

I pray You, loving Jesus, that as You have graciously given me to drink in with delight the words of Your knowledge, so You would mercifully grant me to attain one day to You, the Fountain of all wisdom, and to appear forever before Your face. Amen.

Preface

"Ignorance of the Scriptures
is ignorance of Christ."

-SAINT JEROME

"Learn the heart of God
from the word of God."

-POPE SAINT GREGORY THE GREAT

"It is impossible to rightly govern
the world without God and the Bible."

-GEORGE WASHINGTON

"The Bible is worth all the other books
which have ever been printed."

-PATRICK HENRY

That's a pretty heady list of endorsements. But then, the Word of God does not need human acknowledgement. *You* need God and His Word... now more than ever.

That being said, it can be difficult in your everyday life to find time to read the Scriptures.

Thus, in *Scripture Day by Day*, we offer you a verse or two from the Bible each day, along with a brief meditation or prayer.

Most of the verses are taken from the Church's Liturgical cycle of Readings, to help you connect on a deeper level with the wisdom of Mother Church.

This offering is a daily seed, a seed we trust will grow into a living vine as you use each day's verse and meditation to hopefully springboard into a fuller feasting on God's Word. We strongly encourage you to consider practicing "Lectio Divina" (Divine Reading), a method of reading the Scriptures in such a way as to gradually surrender your own agenda and open yourself to the Spirit of God speaking personally to you through His Word.

In this spirit, then, it is with joy and hope that we offer you *Scripture Day by Day*.

Introduction

Indeed, the word of God is living and effective, sharper than any two-edged sword, penetrating even between soul and spirit, joints and marrow, and able to discern reflections and thoughts of the heart.

-Hebrews 4:12

What's in a word? A word is a vehicle of communication, a means by which we connect with one another. Words inform, command, animate, and question us.

When the word is divine, then it is something more—it's ALIVE! Jesus told us this when He said, "The words I have spoken to you are spirit and life" (John 6:63). Saint Paul reiterated this truth: "Indeed, the word of God is living and effective, sharper than any two-edged sword" (Hebrews 4:12). Thus, we are called to read God's Word in the Holy Scriptures, and to meditate on it, turning it over and over in our hearts. Saint James directs us:

Be doers of the word and not hearers only, deluding yourselves.
For if anyone is a hearer of the word and not a doer, he is like a man
who looks at his own face in a mirror. He sees himself, then goes off and
promptly forgets what he looked like. But the one who peers into the perfect
law of freedom and perseveres, and is not a hearer who forgets but a doer
who acts, such a one shall be blessed in what he does.

-James 1:22-25

We are to *act* on God's Word with faith and obedience. In this way we let the Word sown by the Lord fall on good ground and bear fruit within us, fruit that endures. To avoid this practice is to invite spiritual poverty. As Saint Jerome said, "Ignorance of the Scriptures is ignorance of Christ."

Each of us needs to hear and follow the injunction of Saint Peter: "Like newborn babies, crave pure spiritual milk, so that by it you may grow up in your salvation" (1 Peter 12:2). It is our prayer that these Scriptures will help you connect as deeply as possible with God who is ever present in the hearts of His children, and come to live a life pleasing to Jesus, who is Lord.

In the beginning was the Word,
and the Word was with God,
and the Word was God.
-John 1:1

In the Beginning

Through His Word, God created all that is.
Through you, God wants to restore all things in
Christ Jesus. The Son of God was not alone in His
mission, and neither are you!

JANUARY 2

And Mary kept all these things, reflecting on them in her heart.
-Luke 2:19

Mary

Mary teaches you through her example to receive
God's word and reflect on it, turning it over and
over in your heart. As you begin this new year, pray
for the grace to do just that, and then act on His
Word, as she did. May God be with you.

And the Word became flesh
and made his dwelling among us.
-John 1:14

Word Made Flesh

Saint Athanasius penned this startling truth:
"The Son of God became man so that we might
become God." Are you asking the Lord to become
flesh in you? Are you allowing Him to transform
you into Himself? One of the best ways to do
this is to worship at Holy Mass and receive Holy
Communion often. Then offer yourself back to
Him as a living sacrifice of praise.

But to those who did accept him
he gave power to become children of God.
-John 1:12

Power

We cannot generate ourselves. Only God can give
us power to become His. Have you received His
power? If not, are you willing to ask for it? If you
receive it, are you willing to use it?

Children, let us love not in word or speech but in deed and truth.

-1 John 3:18

In Truth

Jesus would tell us today, "As you act in love, My Spirit will love through you." He seeks love and goodness, faith and works. Today, be the good news to someone in need.

∼ **JANUARY 6** ∼

"We saw his star at its rising and have come to do him homage."

-Matthew 2:2

His Star

The Magi beheld the star of the Messiah. How about you? Have you seen His "star"? If so, do you give Him homage? Do you prostrate yourself in adoration? The Lord tells us, "Be still, and know that I am God."

Upon you the LORD shines,
and over you appears his glory.

-Isaiah 60:2

He Shines

God shines on you and in you! Jesus says, "You are the light of the world today." Trust that He is working through you and go forth with purpose and intention.

In this is love: not that we have loved God,
but that he loved us and sent his Son as expiation for our sins.

-1 John 4:10

His Love

It's good sometimes to remember that God is the initiator of all the good in your life. His love for you is rooted and grounded, not in your emotions, but in His heart—and thus in yours as well. Jesus would tell you today, "I have paid a dear price for you. No one can take you out of my Father's hands."

There is no fear in love, but perfect love drives out fear
because fear has to do with punishment,
and so one who fears is not yet perfect in love.
-1 John 4:18

No Fear

"O Lord, please fill my heart with Your true love, and drive out my fears, doubts, and worries. I can't; You can; and today I let You!"

"The Spirit of the Lord is upon me,
because he has anointed me
to bring glad tidings to the poor.
He has sent me to proclaim liberty to captives
and recovery of sight to the blind,
to let the oppressed go free."
-Luke 4:18

The Spirit of the Lord

"Dear Heavenly Father, Your Spirit was upon Jesus; let it now come upon me. Anoint me to bring good news to the poor, to proclaim true freedom to captives, and recovery of sight to the blind. Give me the grace to help the person imprisoned by sin be set free through an encounter with Jesus!"

"Be made clean."

-Luke 5:13

Would Jesus Heal Me?

It is sometimes difficult to believe that God will heal me, with my own needs, peculiarities, wounds, and sins. But Jesus makes His intention perfectly clear. He says to you today, "I do will your healing. Be made clean!"

We know that no one begotten by God sins; but the one begotten by God he protects, and the evil one cannot touch him.

-1 John 5:18

Untouchable

This is a phenomenal promise to the children of God. God will protect you, if you allow Him, and the evil one cannot touch you. Stay close to God and obey Him, and you will be safe.

So shall my word be
that goes forth from my mouth;
It shall not return to me void,
but shall do my will,
achieving the end for which I sent it.
-Isaiah 55:11

My Purpose

God's Word, which you are reading right now, unlike any other word, has power within itself. Hence it will bring forth a harvest, if only we allow it room to grow in our hearts. It shall not return empty to God, but shall bring forth fruit that remains.

JANUARY 14

"He will baptize you with the holy Spirit and fire."
-Luke 3:16

Fire

God has bigger plans for you than you realize. Ask Him to baptize you with His Holy Spirit. Pray this: "Holy Spirit, set me on fire and teach me today. Come Holy Spirit!"

My strength and my courage is the LORD,
and he has been my savior.
With joy you will draw water
at the fountain of salvation.
-Isaiah 12:2-3

With Joy

God has revealed Himself to you that you might know the joy for which you were created—fellowship with Him. And so, drink from the waters of salvation, in the Sacraments, in prayer, in the Scriptures, in fellowship, in service, and in all the marvelous ways that God provides, with joy!

I will offer a sacrifice of thanksgiving
and call on the name of the LORD.
-Psalm 116:17

Sacrifice of Praise

Sometimes it is indeed a sacrifice to look up from your circumstances, your difficulties, your weaknesses, yes, and even from your sins, and praise the Lord. Yet He is pleased with this sacrifice of trust and worship from His children.

Draw near to God, and he will draw near to you.

-James 4:8

Draw Near

How does one approach the Love that created the cosmos? Thank God, He has revealed the way. Spend time with Him; converse with Him in prayer. Draw near to Him; He will do the rest and you will be blessed!

∽ JANUARY 18 ∽

"This is the time of fulfillment. The kingdom of God is at hand. Repent, and believe in the gospel."

-Mark 1:15

Repent and Believe

Jesus invites you to repent—to turn away from sin—and to believe—to turn to Him in faith. For some, the first step is most difficult; for others, it is the second. Where are you, and more importantly, which step will you choose?

The people were astonished at his teaching, for he taught them as one having authority and not as the scribes.

-Mark 1:22

Authority

The word here for authority is *exousia*, and it means moral authority coupled with power and ability. Have you ever met someone who commands respect just by their very word or attitude? Jesus is that and more. When we follow Him, He imparts His authority to us as well.

∽∾ **JANUARY 20** ∾∽

The LORD makes poor and makes rich,
he humbles, he also exalts.

-1 Samuel 2:7

The Lord

We call Jesus Lord, and so He is. He is in charge; He reigns; all things are in His hands. Wait on Him, and obey Him. You will not be disappointed. They that wait upon the Lord shall renew their strength!

Encourage yourselves daily while it is still "today,"
so that none of you may grow hardened by the deceit of sin.
-Hebrews 3:13

Be Encouraged

Following Jesus is a matter of the heart. It is necessary to work at it, not earning your salvation but cooperating with God's abundant grace. To encourage is to "give heart to"; thus, give heart to someone today, and stay supple, close to God.

∽ **JANUARY 22** ∽

Rise up, help us!
Redeem us as your love demands.
-Psalm 44:27

Redeem Us, Lord

Another translation of this Psalm is: "Redeem us, Lord, because of your mercy." Again, we don't demand this as though we are worthy, but because of our great need and Our Father's great love. As Saint Peter said, "Help me Lord, I'm sinking!"

Therefore, let us strive to enter into that rest,
so that no one may fall after the same example of disobedience.
-Hebrews 4:11

Enter In!

Saint Paul promises us that a "Sabbath rest still remains for the people of God" (Hebrews 4:9). Seek to enter that rest, through a conscious hearkening to and obeying of the voice of God.

∽ **JANUARY 24** ∽

The promises of the LORD I will sing forever,
proclaim your loyalty through all ages.
-Psalm 89:2

Forever I Will Sing

"Forever will I sing your goodness, O Lord! Yes, I decide today that I will extol you O my God, my Father, and the Rock of my salvation! I will call upon You Lord, who are worthy to be praised; so shall I be saved from my enemies."

He fell to the ground and heard a voice saying to him,
"Saul, Saul, why are you persecuting me?"
-Acts 9:4

Why?

Jesus revealed to Saul that He identifies Himself
with His followers. It's as though He told him,
"I am the One you are hurting, or ignoring, or
mistreating." O Lord, help us please to change our
behavior, to let You live more fully through us.

∽ **JANUARY 26** ∽

Then I heard the voice of the Lord saying, "Whom shall I send?
Who will go for us?" "Here I am," I said; "send me!"
-Isaiah 6:8

Send Me!

Let's face it, who is ever entirely equipped to answer
the Lord's call? Even so, He does call. Be willing
to answer Him as best you can, knowing that He
anoints whomever He appoints. "Here I am; send
me!"

*So let us confidently approach the throne of grace to receive mercy
and to find grace for timely help.*

-Hebrews 4:16

Confidently

Don't you love that word, "confidently"? It's a
reminder that you are a child of God, a brother
or sister of Christ Jesus, a conduit of the Holy
Spirit, and an heir of heaven. With this in mind,
renew your flagging spirit, and approach God with
humility, as did Our Blessed Mother Mary.

*"He is the one of whom I said,
'A man is coming after me who ranks ahead of me
because he existed before me.'"*

-John 1:30

Chosen

Jesus will always rank ahead of you. Blessed is the
person who accepts that and chooses to look to
Jesus. He will never let you down. He will lead you
on ways beyond your imagining to blessings beyond
belief. Today, put Jesus first!

They said to him, "Rabbi" (which translated means Teacher),
"where are you staying?" He said to them, "Come, and you will see."
-John 1:38-39

Come and See

You have to start somewhere with Jesus. He says,
"Come and see where I live. Come and spend some
time with me." He will not force you, but He does
invite. Will you RSVP?

∾ **JANUARY 30** ∾

Trust in the LORD with all your heart,
on your own intelligence rely not.
-Proverbs 3:5

Trust in the LORD

God wants you to lean on Him, to trust Him with
your whole heart. The good news is, you don't have
to have all the answers. Beginning today, stop trying
to carry the burden all by yourself. Lean on His
Everlasting Arms.

To each individual the manifestation of the Spirit is given for some benefit.
-1 Corinthians 12:7

The Gifts of the Spirit

God gives the gifts and manifestations of His Holy
Spirit freely to His children, for the good of others.
What gifts has He given you? Are you sharing them
for the benefit of all?

"You have kept the good wine until now."
-John 2:10

Until Now

If it seems like you have been waiting a long time
for the Lord to move in a certain area of your life,
be of good cheer! He often produces His greatest
miracles in the hour of your extreme need. Call out
yet again for His help and deliverance in all your
ways, and get ready for His answers. The best is yet
to come!

Lo, I am sending my messenger
to prepare the way before me;
And suddenly there will come to the temple
the LORD whom you seek.
-Malachi 3:1

Suddenly

Suddenly the Lord comes to His temple. Are you ready to greet Him? If not, now is the time to repent and get right with Him, for He is the Lord of all the earth, and He *is* coming.

"A light for revelation to the Gentiles,
and glory for your people Israel."
-Luke 2:30-32

Revelation and Glory

God prepared His salvation to be the light of the world; have you received His light today? He sent Jesus to be glory for Israel; are you praising Him?

The LORD has sworn and will not waver:
"Like Melchizedek you are a priest forever."
-Psalm 110:4

A Priest Forever

Jesus is our great high priest who has passed
into the heavens. However, it doesn't end there.
Through Baptism, you are also anointed as priest,
to offer spiritual sacrifice for others. You may be the
only Jesus someone will ever meet. Go forth!

"Obedience is better than sacrifice,
and submission than the fat of rams."
-1 Samuel 15:22

Obedience

God is looking for your heart surrendered to Him
in obedience. That means more to Him than any
sacrifice you might choose. One act of surrender
to an unexpected rebuke or ridicule might trump
many self-imposed mortifications. At the end of the
day, who is running your life?

"New wine is poured into fresh wineskins."
-Mark 2:22

New Wineskins

Are you thirsty for more of Jesus? Are you running on empty? Ask Him to give you His new wine, and be ready for the sometimes surprising ways He answers.

"Not as man sees does God see, because man sees the appearance but the LORD looks into the heart."
-1 Samuel 16:7

God Sees

God always seems to get to the heart of the matter, doesn't He? Seek to let go and let God today; take the lower place; to thine own self be true. He knows—and loves—the real you. "That others may be esteemed more than I—Jesus, grant me the grace to desire it."

May the eyes of [your] hearts be enlightened, that you may know
what is the hope that belongs to his call.
-Ephesians 1:18

Open Your Eyes!

Saint Paul prays that God will open the eyes of our hearts, to know Him better. Do you want to see more clearly? Ask Him to give you inner vision. Spend time in Adoration, and listen to His still, small voice, deep in your heart.

For the battle is the LORD'S, and he shall deliver you into our hands."
-1 Samuel 17:47

The Battle

In this passage David testifies that God fights for His people. As then, it is so now. When the battle is upon you, draw near the Lord and cry out for His deliverance. He will defeat the enemies of your soul, and deliver them into your hands.

Blessed be the LORD ...
My safe guard and my fortress,
my stronghold, my deliverer,
My shield, in whom I trust,
who subdues peoples under me.
-Psalm 144:1-2

My Shield

Today God tells you, "I am your stronghold, your fortress, your deliverer. Trust in Me. I will shield you and defend you. Come into My fortress, and I will protect you. Rest and be made strong in Me."

I urge you, brothers, in the name of our Lord Jesus Christ,
that all of you agree in what you say, and that there be no divisions among
you, but that you be united in the same mind and in the same purpose.
-1 Corinthians 1:10

Be United

The Spirit of Jesus within you calls you to agree with your brothers and sisters in the faith. As Saint Augustine is quoted: "In essentials, unity; in non-essentials, liberty; in all things, charity."

"Take care what you hear. The measure with which you measure
will be measured out to you, and still more will be given to you."
-Mark 4:24

God's Measure

God calls us to use what we've been given. If
we do, we will be given more, including more
responsibility! Give generously and in humility. To
God be the glory.

Faith is the realization of what is hoped for
and evidence of things not seen.
-Hebrews 11:1

Faith's Substance

Faith is a substance within you now, the seed
of what is to come: the full and true life of the
Kingdom. Walk in this faith, confident that He
who is within you is always with you, and fortifies
you to act in love.

Love is patient, love is kind.

-1 Corinthians 13:4

True Love

Your new life in Jesus is an exchanged life. He gives you His love with which to love others. But only you can allow Him to love through you. Surrender your irritation and selfishness and let your light shine! Be patient, be gentle; do an unexpected act of kindness today.

[Love] bears all things, believes all things,
hopes all things, endures all things.

-1 Corinthians 13:7

Love True

Love always looks forward, to the One who is love. God said it, I believe it, and that settles it! May His love grow in your heart today, as you give it away.

You have mercy on all, because you can do all things;
and you overlook the sins of men that they may repent.
-Wisdom of Solomon 11:23

Merciful

We must always begin in the embrace of the Father.
God has mercy on all, and overlooks our defects.
Receive His loving-kindness, and begin again.

∽ **FEBRUARY 17** ∽

Rend your hearts, not your garments,
and return to the LORD, your God.
For gracious and merciful is he,
slow to anger, rich in kindness,
and relenting in punishment.
-Joel 2:13

Turn Around

Stop. Just stop and listen. It's time to turn around,
and return with your whole heart to your God.
Think about all He has given you, beginning with
choosing you to be born. He waits for you to come
back home.

*"If anyone wishes to come after me, he must deny himself
and take up his cross daily and follow me."*

-Luke 9:23

Deny Yourself

You have a choice to come after Christ if you so wish. It will mean denying yourself and accepting the cross each day—the responsibilities of your state of life, the difficulties and challenges that arise every day—and doing your best to follow Jesus. But you are not alone; Emmanuel is with you.

Whoever loses his life for my sake will save it.

-Luke 9:24

Save Your Life

Your "yes" to Jesus—your decision to bear the burdens of each day with a smile, with a merciful attitude towards those who might hurt you or bother you or slight you, your decision to prefer others above yourself—all of this frees God up to work it all out to the good!

This, rather, is the fasting that I wish: ...
Sharing your bread with the hungry,
sheltering the oppressed and the homeless;
Clothing the naked when you see them,
and not turning your back on your own.
-Isaiah 58:6-7

True Fasting

In addition to denying ourselves, we are called to donate ourselves to others through acts of mercy, mercifully done. These acts allow God to love His children through us, glorifying Him and blessing others as well.

∼ **FEBRUARY 21** ∼

Then your light shall break forth like the dawn,
and your wound shall quickly be healed.
-Isaiah 58:8

A True Promise

God graciously promises that if you do give of yourself to help another, your own light shall break forth, and your own wound shall be healed. Blessed are the merciful; mercy shall be theirs!

All who call upon me I will answer;
I will be with them in distress;
I will deliver them and give them honor.
-Psalm 91:15

Call Him!

Another translation reads, "When he calls to me, I will answer." God is ready to answer you. He will be with you in trouble; He will deliver you and give you honor. Take Him up on His promise today. Call Him—direct dial!

Restore my joy in your salvation;
sustain in me a willing spirit.
-Psalm 51:14

Restore Me, O Lord!

"Give me back the joy of Your salvation, O Lord!" How deeply we need that joy, that communion, that sense that God delights in us right here and right now! Pray this Psalm with heartfelt longing and faith today that God wants to give you His joy and will do so, soon and very soon.

For just as through the disobedience of one person the many were made sinners, so through the obedience of one the many will be made righteous.

-Romans 5:19

His Gift

His Sacrifice ... for me, saves me this day, in this moment. Through Adam's disobedience and my own sin, I came to know disobedience; through Jesus' obedience, may I come to know grace and peace.

"The Lord, your God, shall you worship and him alone shall you serve."

-Matthew 4:10

God Alone

Jesus returns us to focus and gives us a sure way to defeat temptation: Worship your God, and serve Him. Ask Jesus to help you find in Him what you are looking for in your addictions. Be His!

You shall love your neighbor as yourself. I am the LORD.
-Leviticus 19:18

You Shall Love

Not easy. It takes a decision to move beyond yourself and serve others. Yet when you do so, you access God's love, and He loves through you. Thus His Kingdom comes—through *you*.

∼ **FEBRUARY 27** ∼

"Amen, I say to you, whatever you did for one of these least brothers of mine, you did for me."
-Matthew 25:40

"You Did It for Me."

"You did it for Me." Wow. There it is. So simple, yet ... so easy to step around. Let us take God at His word, and, as Pope Francis teaches us, "try a little harder" ... to serve, to smile, to give, to love.

"This is how you are to pray:
Our Father in heaven,
hallowed be your name."
-Matthew 6:9

Abba

Our Father. Just think about that for a moment. You have a Father in heaven. Not a Landlord, or a Drill Instructor, or even a benevolent Dictator, but a Father. A Father who loves you. How about taking five and just visiting with Him ... now? Begin with praise. Hallow His Name.

∽ **FEBRUARY 29** ∼

Cast away from you all the crimes you have committed,
and make for yourselves a new heart and a new spirit.
Why should you die, O house of Israel?
-Ezekiel 18:31

A New Heart

Many times you have perhaps stopped committing a certain sin or giving in to a particular habit. The problem is not in stopping, but rather in not starting it up again! Cast away from you all your crimes, and ask God for a new spirit. Only He can make you holy, and whole.

Go first and be reconciled with your brother,
and then come and offer your gift.

-Matthew 5:24

Be Reconciled

Jesus knows how easily you can be deceived into living on the outside, to keeping up appearances. He calls you always back to your heart, to the real issue. As C.S. Lewis said, "Integrity is doing the right thing even when no one is watching."

Today the LORD is making this agreement with you:
you are to be a people peculiarly his own, as he promised you.

-Deuteronomy 26:18

Agreement

We are a peculiar people, and peculiarly the Lord's. Think about that. You are held in the hands of the Lord God of the Cosmos. You belong to Him! Therefore, keep up your part of the covenant. Today, give yourself again to Him.

*Bear your share of hardship for the gospel
with the strength that comes from God.*
-2 Timothy 1:8

Bear Your Share

It's going to be hard at times to follow Jesus, to proclaim His Gospel, to obey His Word. Yet Saint Paul shows you a secret: endure with the strength that comes from God! That way you can rejoice in spirit. As Saint Catherine of Siena said, "It's heaven all the way to heaven."

∽ **MARCH 4** ∽

*While he was still speaking, behold, a bright cloud cast a shadow over
them, then from the cloud came a voice that said,*
"This is my beloved Son, with whom I am well pleased; listen to him."
-Matthew 17:5

I Am Well Pleased

God affirmed His Son. In Christ, you are also God's adopted and beloved child. Receive His affirmation as you trust in the finished work of Calvary and follow God by your cooperation with the Holy Spirit. Listen to Him!

Our citizenship is in heaven, and from it we also await a savior,
the Lord Jesus Christ.
-Philippians 3:20

A Citizen of Heaven

Stop. Realize that you are a citizen of heaven ...
right now! Your Father delights in you and is
working all things for your good, and your Savior
will come from heaven when all is ready.

Forgive and you will be forgiven.
-Luke 6:37

Forgive and You Will Be Forgiven

"Dear God, please help me to stop judging and
comparing myself to others. Help me to realize
that You know me and love me for who I am—Your
child. I can then reach out to love others, and offer
them the same gift You give me: eternal life. In
Jesus' name. Amen."

Learn to do good.
Make justice your aim: redress the wronged,
hear the orphan's plea, defend the widow.

-Isaiah 1:17

Learn to Do Good

"No one is born learnt." Isaiah urges you today to have a teachable spirit, and to respond to the wrongs you see and the pleas you hear. Defend those who have no voice. Help those who have been defrauded. Learn to do good.

I will praise you, LORD, with all my heart;
I will declare all your wondrous deeds.
I will delight and rejoice in you;
I will sing hymns to your name, Most High.

-Psalm 9:2-3

Praise Him!

Take a moment today and just tell God that you delight in Him. Rejoice in Him, the Maker of heaven and earth. Even if you don't feel like praising Him, do so by faith. God is listening and He loves your worship. He inhabits the praises of His people.

Whoever exalts himself will be humbled;
but whoever humbles himself will be exalted.
-Matthew 23:12

Stay Low

Do you like to be noticed? It's pretty normal. Jesus tells us that the key is to surrender that desire and to choose instead to be low, to serve. As the saying goes, "It's nice to be important, but it's more important to be nice!"

∽◦◦ **MARCH 10** ◦◦∽

Blessed is the man who trusts in the LORD,
whose hope is the LORD.
He is like a tree planted beside the waters
that stretches out its roots to the stream.
-Jeremiah 17:7-8

Trust in the Lord

Ah, the gift of trusting in the Lord! Blessed indeed are you when you put your trust in the Lord, and decide to rest in Him. Let your roots go down deep into the rivers of Life, and let God's vitality flow through you ever more. "Jesus, I trust in You."

"Your brother was dead and has come to life again;
he was lost and has been found."
-Luke 15:32

Found

In the parable of the Prodigal Son, are you more
like the younger son, the elder brother, or the
father? Who is wandering or returning, dutiful or
resentful, grieving or rejoicing, in your life today?
What is Jesus asking of you?

Therefore, since we have been justified by faith, we have peace with God
through our Lord Jesus Christ, through whom we have gained access
[by faith] to this grace in which we stand,
and we boast in hope of the glory of God.
-Romans 5:1-2

Justified

We are justified. It's good sometimes just to stop
and remember that. You have been saved; you are
being saved; you hope to be saved. Jesus has won
access for us to the grace of God, and this grace
gives us excitement about the future, where we hope
to share in the glory of God. Are you excited?

"Whoever drinks the water I shall give will never thirst; the water I shall give will become in him a spring of water welling up to eternal life."
-John 4:14

Thirsty?

This is an exciting promise! Not only does Jesus give you a drink, He promises to gives you a spring that wells up to eternal life. Is your faucet open, or has the pump gone a bit dry? If so, now is the time to ask Him to open up the dam and let the river flow!

"Remember to keep holy the sabbath day."
-Exodus 20:8

Keep Holy the Sabbath

On the seventh day the Lord rested; He directs you to do the same. It is a day holy unto Him. Give yourself and your loved ones the gift of obedient rest. Honor the Lord on the first day and you will realize His blessings the rest of the week as well. Remember to keep holy the Sabbath.

"Zeal for your house will consume me."
-John 2:17

Consuming Zeal

Finally Jesus has had enough. It's like the callousness and apathy of God's chosen people reaches its peak, and He lets go. How about you? Are you eager for the things of God, or have you lost your zest? If the latter, seek the Lord while He may be found, and beg Him for a new heart. Be consumed with zeal. Be eager for God!

*"Come no nearer! Remove the sandals from your feet,
for the place where you stand is holy ground."*
-Exodus 3:5

Holy Ground

God draws near to you out of His consuming love, yet He remains who He is: the Holy God of Israel, surrounded by Shekinah glory. Like Moses, remove your sandals, draw near in holy adoration, worship the Lord, and wait upon Him.

"Sir, leave it for this year also, and I shall cultivate the ground around it and fertilize it; it may bear fruit in the future. If not you can cut it down."
-Luke 13:8-9

A Second Chance

The Lord is merciful—full of mercy. He looks for fruit from you. If you fear you have little or no fruit to show Him, now is the time to return to Him and beg Him to fill you with His precious Holy Spirit. Now is the time to accept His gracious allowance and to respond. He is the God of the second chance, but you have to act!

As the deer longs for streams of water,
so my soul longs for you, O God.
-Psalm 42:2

As a Deer

Saint Augustine wrote, "God thirsts that we may thirst for Him." O Lord, help us to hunger after You, to long for you, to thirst for You. Show us Your face, O Lord, and that will be enough. Draw us to Thy side, and never let us be parted from You."

Joseph her husband ... was a righteous man.

-Matthew 1:19

A Righteous Man

Joseph, the husband of Mary, was a sincere, humble, and upright man, of authentic moral character. Joseph's obedience to God and His ways did not shield him from temptation and trial, but it did deliver him, as it will us. Let us ask his intercession to be truly chaste and humbly upright.

*"But with contrite heart and humble spirit
let us be received."*

-Daniel 3:39

A Contrite Heart

It can be difficult to admit you're at fault, and even responsible, for wrong decisions, wrong beliefs, wrong judgements. However, it is a necessary step towards contrition and conversion. Don't hold back; admit your brokenness, and then come forward to be accepted, by the One who came for this very purpose, that you might repent and be saved.

*Moved with compassion the master of that servant let him go
and forgave him the loan.*
-Matthew 18:27

Loan Forgiveness

Moved with compassion, the Lord has forgiven you
of all you owe Him. That's hard to grasp for many
people. Forgiven. Totally cleansed, of all your acts of
lust, pride, disobedience, and selfishness ... all your
sin. He says to you today, "Go in peace. Your sins
are forgiven."

∽ **MARCH 22** ∽

Should you not have had pity on your fellow servant, as I had pity on you?'
·Matthew 18:33

Pay it Forward

As you are blessed by forgiveness, so bless others.
Be quick to extend mercy, be it with a smile or a
helping hand, or a forgiving word. Guard against a
hardened heart or a complaining spirit.

LORD, who may abide in your tent?
Who may dwell on your holy mountain?
Whoever walks without blame,
doing what is right,
speaking truth from the heart.
-Psalm 15:1-2

Who May Abide?

Do you want to live with God and abide in His "tent"? Then ask Him for the grace to walk blamelessly and do the right. Speak less, love more.

"Now, Israel, hear the statutes and decrees which I am teaching you to observe, that you may live, and may enter in and take possession of the land which the LORD, the God of your fathers, is giving you."
-Deuteronomy 4:1

Enter In

God has a plan for you, an inheritance He wants you to possess. Thus, He calls you to listen to and observe His commands, which are not burdensome, but are words of life. Today, ask for the grace to do His Will.

And coming to her, he said, "Hail, favored one! The Lord is with you."
-Luke 1:28

The Lord is With You

The Lord is always the one who initiates. Today, He sends Gabriel to announce to Mary that He has chosen her to be the mother of His Son. He says to you, "You are also my chosen. Listen to Me and follow Me. I have work for you to do."

∽ **MARCH 26** ∽

Mary said, "Behold, I am the handmaid of the Lord.
May it be done to me according to your word."
-Luke 1:38

Fiat

Mary surrendered to the Lord both passively and actively. She allowed Him to work within her, unimpeded by her self-will. She also cooperated with Him, to the best of her ability, teaching us we need both movements in our life.

Whoever is not with me is against me,
and whoever does not gather with me scatters.
-Luke 11:23

With or Against?

Once you have yielded your heart to Jesus and received Him as your Savior, you have a commission. You, along with all members of the Church, are called to mission: to invite all people into the communion of love shared by the Blessed Trinity. Passivity is not an option.

∽ **MARCH 28** ∾

All the nations you have made shall come
to bow before you, Lord,
and give honor to your name.
For you are great and do wondrous deeds;
and you alone are God.
-Psalm 86:9-10

You Alone

God. His greatness is unsearchable. Take a moment and praise Him today. He goes ahead of you; He is behind you. He is within you and yet outside of you. He is the great "I Am!" He alone is God!

"'To love him with all your heart, with all your understanding,
with all your strength, and to love your neighbor as yourself'
is worth more than all burnt offerings and sacrifices."
-Mark 12:33

Love

To love Him. To love others. To love. Saint Therese of Lisieux wrote, "Merit does not consist in doing or giving much. It consists in loving much."

"Come, let us return to the LORD,
For it is he who has rent, but he will heal us;
he has struck us, but he will bind our wounds."
-Hosea 6:1

He Will Heal

Only God can heal us. Thank God, He has promised to do this very thing. Let us do our part. Let us return to Him, let us seek to know Him; let us spend time alone with Him. "For it is love that I desire, not sacrifice, and knowledge of God rather than holocausts" (Hosea 6:6).

MARCH 31

The God of all grace who called you to his eternal glory through Christ [Jesus] will himself restore, confirm, strengthen, and establish you after you have suffered a little. To him be dominion forever. Amen.

-1 Peter 5:10-11

A Little Suffering

It's normal to want to avoid suffering. But God knows that suffering, or enduring hardship, has a way of burning up evil, of deepening us, of grounding us in reality. The good news is, Jesus Himself will restore us afterwards. So hold on! To Him be dominion forever.

APRIL 1

"Awake, O sleeper,
and arise from the dead,
and Christ will give you light."

-Ephesians 5:14

Wake Up!

The Lord would tell you today, "Try to learn what pleases Me. Take no part in the works of darkness but rather expose them. Wake up! Arise and receive My Light."

Then Jesus said, "I came into this world for judgment, so that those who do not see might see, and those who do see might become blind."
-John 9:39

Judgment

For those who cannot see, like the blind man in today's reading, Jesus comes to give sight. For those who claim to see, like the Pharisees, Jesus withholds the true light, that they might perhaps search for it, and find life.

Jesus told her, "I am the resurrection and the life; whoever believes in me, even if he dies, will live."
-John 11:25

Life

It really is a great relief to know that our hope is outside of us, that when we sin or make a mistake, that's not the end of it. Jesus is our Resurrection. He alone has the power to constantly renew our inner spirit with faith, hope, and sincere love.

Amen, amen, I say to you, unless a grain of wheat falls to the
ground and dies, it remains just a grain of wheat;
but if it dies, it produces much fruit.
-John 12:24

From Death to Life

Jesus plainly tells us we have to die to ourselves, yet
not without hope. In surrendering we will find new
life—but it might take a while. Be patient with all
that is yet to be. All growth is gradual.

∽ **APRIL 5** ∽

See, I am doing something new!
Now it springs forth, do you not perceive it?
In the desert I make a way,
in the wasteland, rivers.
-Isaiah 43:19

Something New

It is precisely when we are in the desert, in the
difficult and seemingly boxed-in places in our lives,
that God promises to make a way, an escape, a
solution. God doesn't so much solve problems as
dis-solve them. He is supremely creative yet gentle.
Re-read this verse and be encouraged. When you're
down to nothing, God's up to something!

"Say to daughter Zion,
'Behold, your king comes to you,
meek and riding on an ass,
and on a colt, the foal of a beast of burden.'"
-Matthew 21:5

A Beast of Burden

The humility of God in His Son Jesus is a ceaseless wonder. With His divine power under restraint, He comes to us as the One who will bear our burdens. What people has such a God as this? Likewise, when you feel overwhelmed, remember this.

∾ **APRIL 7** ∾

The Lord GOD is my help,
therefore I am not disgraced;
I have set my face like flint,
knowing that I shall not be put to shame.
-Isaiah 50:7

Like Flint

"Trust in Me today," the Lord tells you. "Do not try to plan out the future, but rather focus on Me in this moment; set the face of your soul towards Me, and trust." Ask Mary, Help of Christians, to intercede for you.

"Remain here and keep watch with me."
-Matthew 26:38

Watch!

The Lord calls you to watch one hour with Him ... this can be at church, in Adoration, at home ... but the key is to watch, to wait, to be attentive. Jesus has much to tell you, much to teach you. Watch with Him, and wait on Him, so you can walk with Him.

"From now on you will see 'the Son of Man seated at the right hand of the Power' and 'coming on the clouds of heaven.'"
-Matthew 26:64

Coming in Power

Every eye will see Jesus when He returns in glory with all the angels. Rejected by men, He ever lives as the glorious Son of God. Be consoled and encouraged with this truth. Ask Jesus to give you His power today to calm your soul and guide your steps.

"Eli, Eli, lema sabachthani?" which means,
"My God, my God, why have you forsaken me?"
-Matthew 27:46

"Eli, Eli, lema sabachthani?"

Forsaken. It's a terrible feeling. Yet Jesus truly felt it, as He hung bereft on the cross, abandoned for your sake. Today, trust in Him. Trust that He knows all you are feeling, and He is with you, to deliver you. His unfailing love will raise you up.

When Jesus had taken the wine, he said, "It is finished."
And bowing his head, he handed over the spirit.
-John 19:30

"It Is Finished."

"It is finished." The salvation of the world has been won. The enemy has been defeated. The gates of heaven are opened. Our mighty champion has done all this ... for you. Today, receive Jesus' definitive victory in your soul, and live it!

"Do not be afraid! I know that you are seeking Jesus the crucified.
He is not here, for he has been raised just as he said."
-Matthew 28:5-6

Do Not Be Afraid!

It is the morning of the Resurrection. Like the women, we too have been seeking Jesus, who sometimes seems to be far from us. But let us take courage. He is risen, as He said! He will be found by us if we look for Him.

~ APRIL 13 ~

"Then go quickly and tell his disciples, 'He has been raised from the dead,
and he is going before you to Galilee.'"
-Matthew 28:7

Go and Tell

God could have infused the knowledge of the Resurrection in the minds of His disciples, but He chose instead to use the faithful and courageous women as His messengers. Similarly, He calls *you* to bring His good news to others. Ask for the grace to share Jesus with someone today. It's His way.

This is the day the LORD has made;
let us rejoice in it and be glad.

-Psalm 118:24

This Is the Day

This is the day the Lord has made. You can let go
and enjoy it, because you're not in charge! The
Lord made you, and all that has to do with you. So
rejoice today, and be glad. You are in His hands and
you are in His Heart. He is Risen!

If then you were raised with Christ, seek what is above,
where Christ is seated at the right hand of God.

-Colossians 3:1

Seek What Is Above

You are a new creation, if you have received Jesus
and been baptized. You have been raised from
death with Him. Seek the things of heaven, and
heaven will come to you. As C.S. Lewis once aptly
noted, "Aim at heaven, and you'll get earth thrown
in; aim at earth, and you'll get neither."

Therefore let us celebrate the feast,
not with the old yeast, the yeast of malice and wickedness,
but with the unleavened bread of sincerity and truth.
-1 Corinthians 5:8

The Old Yeast

We really do need to get rid of all malevolence in our hearts, and only Jesus can cleanse us. The Sacrament of Reconciliation is the primary means in which to do this. Clear out the old yeast today!

'You have made known to me the paths of life;
you will fill me with joy in your presence.'
-Acts 2:28

You Will Fill Me with Joy!

The Lord shows you the path of life. "Walk this way," He says. If you do, you can be assured He will also fill you with His joy, a joy so deep in your heart!

But the LORD'S eyes are upon the reverent,
upon those who hope for his gracious help,
Delivering them from death,
keeping them alive in times of famine.
-Psalm 33:18-19

Deliverance!

Sometimes you may feel you are no longer in God's sight, but that's simply not true. His eyes are ever upon those who fear Him and hope in Him. Stay true; He will deliver you!

But they urged him, "Stay with us, for it is nearly evening
and the day is almost over." So he went in to stay with them.
-Luke 24:29

Stay with Us

In this poignant moment of twilight, the disciples beg Jesus to stay with them. How utterly human. Life somehow seems more nostalgic at sunset, a sign perhaps of our own impending departure. Jesus obliges. How utterly divine. What a mighty God we serve!

Everyone who does not listen to that prophet will be cut off from the people.

-Acts 3:23

Listen!

There are serious consequences to our free will. Once we hear God, we are obliged to obey Him, to seek Him. There is no "pass" card when it comes to life. Are you listening to Jesus? Are you acting on His word?

∾ APRIL 21 ∾

Yet you have made them little less than a god,
crowned them with glory and honor.

-Psalm 8:5

Crowned

Do you know that you are fearfully and wonderfully made? You are the apple of God's eye, created a little less than a god. Receive the Scriptural truth about yourself, and be the blessing God created you to be!

You are "a chosen race, a royal priesthood, a holy nation,
a people of his own, so that you may announce the praises" of him
who called you out of darkness into his wonderful light.

-1 Peter 2:9

His

Just think, God has claimed you as His own! You belong to Him now. Just let that realization sink into your soul. You are not orphaned. He has called you into His marvelous light, and He has work for you to do: to announce His praise!

≈ **APRIL 23** ≈

He led them on secure and unafraid,
but the sea enveloped their enemies.

-Psalm 78:53

Protected

God promises to keep us secure. However, those who do not receive Him have no such hope. Let us ask God to give us a desire to share Him with all we meet, that they can be safe as well.

"Cast the net over the right side of the boat and you will find something."
So they cast it, and were not able to pull it in
because of the number of fish.
-John 21:6

Keep Fishing!

Have you ever felt like giving up in your walk with the Lord? DON'T! The apostles had been fishing all night, but when Jesus gave the word, the catch was overwhelming. Keep fishing!

~~~ **APRIL 25** ~~~

The LORD chastised me harshly,
but did not hand me over to death.
-Psalm 118:18

Scolded but Not Slain

God allows you to experience some of the consequences of your misdeeds. He uses these very circumstances to remold you into His image. This can take some time. Yet, as Saint Teresa of Avila said, "God never withholds Himself from the soul that perseveres." Be of good cheer. You will rise again!

Like newborn infants, long for pure spiritual milk
so that through it you may grow into salvation.
-1 Peter 2:2

Pure Milk

God wants us to long for Him, to hunger and thirst
for Him. Think of yourself as a newborn baby,
hungry for nourishment. Come to Him and drink.
Receive the sacraments, be filled with His Spirit.
He also longs for you!

～ APRIL 27 ～

They devoted themselves to the teaching of the apostles
and to the communal life, to the breaking of the bread and to the prayers.
-Acts 2:42

A Good Diet

It is good to reflect on the essentials of our Church,
the community of believers, from the beginning:
Scripture, Fellowship, the Eucharist, and Prayer.
Are you including these in your diet of faith? As the
saying goes, "You are what you eat!"

Give thanks to the LORD, who is good,
whose love endures forever.
Let the house of Israel say:
God's love endures forever.
-Psalm 118:1-2

Give Thanks

Let not only the house of Israel thank God, but let your household thank God too! Everything you have is gift...your life, your health, your livelihood, your loved ones, your home, your provisions, and most of all, your eternal life.

⤳ APRIL 29 ⤳

Although you have not seen him you love him; even though you do not see him now yet believe in him, you rejoice with an indescribable and glorious joy, as you attain the goal of [your] faith, the salvation of your souls.
-1 Peter 1:8-9

You Love Him

Today just stop and realize that you are loved. God appreciates your desire to love Him and serve Him in others. Rejoice that He is bringing you step by step into union with Himself. Even now, He is one with your spirit. Deo Gratias.

Whoever is begotten by God conquers the world.
And the victory that conquers the world is our faith.

-1 John 5:4

Victory!

You are more than a conqueror in God. You may not always feel that, but it is true nonetheless. We walk by faith, not by sight. Ask God to deepen your faith in the victory already won. Then go forth and conquer!

∽≈ **MAY 1** ≈∽

All these devoted themselves with one accord to prayer,
together with some women, and Mary the mother of Jesus, and his brothers.

-Acts 1:14

Mary

Mary is with us always, to help bring us to her Son Jesus. Just as she joined the disciples in prayer, she also joins you. Through the Rosary especially may you come to know her powerful motherly intercession. Our Mother, our confidence, pray for us, now and at the hour of our death. Amen.

I, John, your brother, who share with you the distress, the kingdom, and the
endurance we have in Jesus, found myself on the island called Patmos
because I proclaimed God's word and gave testimony to Jesus.
-Revelation 1:9

Endure

By grace, you are united with Saint John, the
beloved disciple, and share with him and all
believers the joys and sufferings of being part of the
Body of Christ. Pray that all may withstand until
the end, and inherit eternal life!

∞ **MAY 3** ∞

"Do not be afraid. I am the first and the last, the one who lives.
Once I was dead, but now I am alive forever and ever.
I hold the keys to death and the netherworld."
-Revelation 1:17-18

Assurance

C. S. Lewis wrote of Aslan in *The Chronicles of*
Narnia, "He's wild, you know. Not like a tame lion."
The Lord we serve is glorious in His power over all
evil. Ask Him to help you today, and rest assured of
His presence. He is alive forever!

He breathed on them and said to them, "Receive the holy Spirit.
Whose sins you forgive are forgiven them,
and whose sins you retain are retained."
-John 20:22-23

Forgiven

Knowing we would need forgiveness always, Jesus
left us a powerful Sacrament of His mercy. In
Confession, we can know without a doubt that
He absolves us from all our sins, heals us, and
strengthens us in our battle to be holy.

∞ **MAY 5** ∞

Now Jesus did many other signs in the presence of [his] disciples that are
not written in this book. But these are written that you may [come to]
believe that Jesus is the Messiah, the Son of God,
and that through this belief you may have life in his name.
-John 20:30-31

Believe and Receive

God gave us the Gospels to help you believe that
Jesus is Lord, and through this belief to receive life.
Therefore, live in such a way as to glorify God.

And when they heard it, they raised their voices to God with one accord.

-Acts 4:24

In One Accord

The early Church was united in their need of God and in their resultant cry to Him. With whom do you pray in one accord? God delights in our union with Him and one another.

∽ **MAY 7** ∾

"Amen, amen, I say to you, no one can enter the kingdom of God without being born of water and Spirit."

-John 3:5

Water and Spirit

Baptismal water cleanses us and the Holy Spirit inbreathes us with a new life. God invites us to enter His kingdom, to see with new eyes. The life of faith is a daring adventure. Are you in?

"The wind blows where it wills, and you can hear the sound it makes,
but you do not know where it comes from or where it goes;
so it is with everyone who is born of the Spirit."

-John 3:8

Spirit Wind

Do you want more of God in your life? Surrender. Surrender to His Holy Spirit, to the heavenly wind that blows across your soul. God wants to move ... in you!

∽ **MAY 9** ∽

There was no needy person among them.

-Acts 4:34

All In

This is a phenomenal reality. Not one person in the early Church was "on the periphery." Each cared for the other, and laid their goods out for all. They could only do this because they felt the deep love of God moving them to hold all things in common. How is God asking you to be merciful today?

MAY 10

In all your ways be mindful of him,
and he will make straight your paths.
-Proverbs 3:6

Straight Paths

God doesn't want to control us, but to walk with us, to guide us, to counsel us, to enjoy the adventure with us. Today, acknowledge God in all your ways, wait for His direction, and act on it!

MAY 11

Your decrees are firmly established;
holiness belongs to your house, LORD,
for all the length of days.
-Psalm 93:5

Holiness

Today You can trust in God, because He is trustworthy. His decrees are sure. His house is holy. If you feel small or lowly, put your hand in His. He will raise you up. "For my house shall be called a house of prayer for all peoples" (Isaiah 56:7).

"Was it not necessary that the Messiah should suffer these things and enter into his glory?"

-Luke 24:26

Necessary

All of life involves dying and rising. Even Jesus learned obedience from what he suffered. Let us likewise be not dismayed when we encounter suffering, but rather let us praise God and continue on in hope. His ways are not our ways, nor are our thoughts His thoughts. Yet He knows what is best in the end.

～ **MAY 13** ～

His mother said to the servers, "Do whatever he tells you."

-John 2:5

Listen up!

There may be many voices calling you, many distractions "tugging at your sleeve" today. However, like a good mother, Mary reminds you of the one essential. Listen and obey.

The LORD is close to the brokenhearted,
saves those whose spirit is crushed.

-Psalm 34:19

Close

It has been said that when the world rushes out, the Lord rushes in. Jesus knows what it is to bear great, pressing sorrow. He and He alone, can heal a broken heart. Invite Him into yours today, and reach out to see how you can be His presence to someone else.

Learn to savor how good the LORD is;
happy are those who take refuge in him.

-Psalm 34:9

How good!

Jesus' greatest gift to you is His Body, His Blood, His Soul, and His Divinity—Himself—in the Holy Eucharist. It would take an eternity to begin to experience the fullness of this gift, yet it is yours today. So do yourself an eternal favor. Go to Mass, worship the Lord—Taste and see!

Now if you invoke as Father him who judges impartially
according to each one's works, conduct yourselves with
reverence during the time of your sojourning.
-1 Peter 1:17

Good Conduct

You are here on earth for only a short while. You belong to the Creator of the Cosmos, and your eternal home is beyond, with Him, in eternity. Hence, be reverent and God-centered while you are away.

∽∾ MAY 17 ∽∾

Then they said to each other, "Were not our hearts burning [within us]
while he spoke to us on the way and opened the scriptures to us?"
-Luke 24:32

An Ardent Heart

Jesus often surprises us, as Pope Francis says, with His presence and unexpected encounters. But our hearts tell us much if we can be sensitive to them. Try praying when your heart speaks to you, and listen when you feel it burning within you.

MAY 18

If anyone does sin, we have an Advocate with the Father,
Jesus Christ the righteous one.
-1 John 2:1

An Advocate

It is truly good news to know we have an Advocate in this litigious world, someone who speaks on our behalf to the Father. Today, be encouraged. Confess your sin and live!

MAY 19

"We are witnesses of these things, as is the holy Spirit
that God has given to those who obey him."
-Acts 5:32

Witnesses

"The duty of Christians to take part in the life of the Church impels them to act as witnesses of the Gospel." (Catholic Catechism # 2742) Indeed, God has given us His Spirit to empower us to be the good news to one another, through the Spirit of Christ living within us.

You changed my mourning into dancing;
you took off my sackcloth
and clothed me with gladness.
With my whole being I sing
endless praise to you.
O LORD, my God,
forever will I give you thanks.
-Psalm 30:12-13

Endless Thanksgiving

Only when you have been set free from sorrow
and clothed with gladness can you sing with your
whole being. Trust that God is doing this very thing
within you. Begin singing today!

"Worthy is the Lamb that was slain
to receive power and riches, wisdom and strength,
honor and glory and blessing."
-Revelation 5:12

Worthy

Worthy indeed is Jesus our Redeemer, the precious
Lamb of God. He was slain for us, yet now He lives.
Today, meditate on this great truth, and pray to be
found worthy to stand when He returns.

"When you grow old, you will stretch out your hands, and someone else will
dress you and lead you where you do not want to go."
-John 21:18

Dying and Rising

So it is in this life that along with the anointing
comes adversity. However, you can still trust the
Lord always, because Jesus will never leave you nor
forsake you. He will give you what you need when
you need it. Trust in Him.

"For the bread of God is that which comes down from heaven
and gives life to the world."
-John 6:33

Life for the World

Sometimes we fail to let God's incredible truth
disarm us. Every time we receive the Eucharist we
receive the Life of the world! Every time we ask
Jesus into our hearts we receive the Bread of God.
Thank You dear God for being so good!

For unclean spirits, crying out in a loud voice,
came out of many possessed people,
and many paralyzed and crippled people were cured.
-Acts 8:7

Deliverance!

Jesus unleashed the mighty power of God on earth,
and He gave us this same power. Believe that God
wants to use *you*, and ask Him to release His power
in you, that you might bring hope and deliverance
to His world.

∽ **MAY 25** ∽

Whoever eats my flesh and drinks my blood remains in me and I in him.
-John 6:56

True Life

True union is to abide in God, and to have God
abide in you. Here is the promise Jesus gives you.
This is eternal life, right here and right now. It is
both a deep peace and an active concern for the
good of others—a concern that moves you to action.

It is the spirit that gives life, while the flesh is of no avail.
The words I have spoken to you are spirit and life.

-John 6:63

Spirit and Life

We are totally dependent on God's grace. His Spirit gives life, not your efforts. However, you must make the effort to seek Him! Ask God to grant that you might come to better know His Son.

The LORD is my shepherd;
there is nothing I lack.

-Psalm 23:1

My Shepherd

You have a Shepherd. That means you qualify as one His beloved sheep! Claim this promise today, that you lack nothing when you are His.

For you had gone astray like sheep,
but you have now returned to the shepherd and guardian of your souls.
-1 Peter 2:25

Safe!

Sheep have a penchant for being easily led astray. That's why they need a shepherd! If you feel a little lost today, return to the Shepherd of you soul and stay close to His side, forever.

∽ **MAY 29** ∽

I am the gate. Whoever enters through me will be saved,
and will come in and go out and find pasture.
-John 10:9

The Gate

Whenever you find yourself unsure about a decision, stop. Seek the Lord. He is the gate through whom you must go in and out. HE will lead you to a good pasture, in His own good time.

A thief comes only to steal and slaughter and destroy.
-John 10:10

A Thief

Whenever you see any of the three things mentioned in this verse happening in your life, take note. Jesus is exposing their source. Rebuke the devil and he will flee.

I came so that they might have life and have it more abundantly.
-John 10:10

A Giver

Conversely to yesterday's word, the true Shepherd comes only to give us life, and to give it more and more. God wants us to grow rich in His Spirit and grace. As Saint Irenaeus said, "The glory of God is man fully alive!"

"You will receive power when the holy Spirit comes upon you, and you will
be my witnesses in Jerusalem, throughout Judea and Samaria,
and to the ends of the earth."

-Acts 1:8

Power

Jesus promises to give you His power, a power won for you through His Death and Resurrection. Ask for this power and accept it, so that you can be His witness wherever you go!

That the God of our Lord Jesus Christ, the Father of glory, may give you a
spirit of wisdom and revelation resulting in knowledge of him.

Ephesians 1:17

Revelation

Saint Paul prays that God will give us wisdom (practical understanding) and revelation (spiritual insight) in the knowledge of Him. Ask God to help you receive and walk in both His natural and supernatural light today.

May the eyes of [your] hearts be enlightened,
that you may know what is the hope that belongs to his call,
what are the riches of glory in his inheritance among the holy ones.
-Ephesians 1:18

I Have a Hope!

God wants you to have hope in your heart this day, a hope grounded in the truth that He has called you and you belong to Him. You are His, now and forever. Praise and thank Him now!

And he put all things beneath his feet and gave him as head over
all things to the church, which is his body,
the fullness of the one who fills all things in every way.
-Ephesians 1:22-23

Under His Feet

When you struggle with a difficulty, it can be easy to forget that everything in your life is under the feet of Jesus, that He already has it under control. Today, pause for a moment and meditate on this truth. Put your hand in the hand of the Man from Galilee!

"He ascended on high and took prisoners captive;
he gave gifts to men."

-Ephesians 4:8

Gifts and Giftings

Jesus did not just come to visit and wish us well.
He has a plan and purpose for you. He has gifts to
give you. Ask Him to both give you His gifts and to
reveal to you His giftings at work in you, that you
might use them and bear fruit that remains.

Until we all attain to the unity of faith and knowledge of the Son of God,
to mature manhood, to the extent of the full stature of Christ.

-Ephesians 4:13

Together

God is developing a people who will together reach
a unity in the faith and in the knowledge of the Son
of God, and manifest His presence to the world.
This is a fascinating truth that will become more
apparent as you follow Jesus.

When the time for Pentecost was fulfilled, they were all in one place together. And suddenly there came from the sky a noise like a strong driving wind, and it filled the entire house in which they were.

-Acts 2:1-2

Fulfillment

The disciples and Mary were all together in one place. Suddenly, God moved. The Spirit descended like a strong, pushing wind, filling the entire house—and all who were in it!

Then there appeared to them tongues as of fire, which parted and came to rest on each one of them. And they were all filled with the holy Spirit and began to speak in different tongues, as the Spirit enabled them to proclaim.

-Acts 2:3-4

Tongues of Fire

The Holy Spirit, separated from us since the fall of our first parents, now returns with passion and fervor to give us new life! On that glorious morning, God and man enjoyed a true reunion, one that continues to this very day. Have you received the Holy Spirit?

When you send forth your breath, they are created,
and you renew the face of the earth.

-Psalm 104:30

Come Holy Spirit!

The Holy Spirit has come to renew and make beautiful the face of the earth. Take some quiet time just to be with God for a few moments today. Let Him renew you.

∽∾ JUNE 10 ∽∾

To each individual the manifestation of the Spirit is given for some benefit.

1 Corinthians 12:7

The Common Good

"To each person the gift of the Spirit is given for the common good." That means you must not hold on to your gifts, but rather share them. If you do, both you and others will find eternal life. If you do not, the Body of Christ will be less for that. How will you choose?

∽ JUNE 11 ∽

I will sing to the LORD all my life;
I will sing praise to my God while I live.
May my theme be pleasing to God;
I will rejoice in the LORD.
-Psalm 104:33-34

I will sing!

The Psalmist states it clearly: "I will rejoice in the Lord." This is how you are also invited to voice your faith. Faith is a choice; love is an act. God bless you!

∽ JUNE 12 ∽

Live by the Spirit and you will certainly not gratify the desire of the flesh.
-Galatians 5:16

By the Spirit

Saint Paul gives us the secret to a victorious life: live by the Spirit. The Lord leads; the devil drives. Let the Spirit lead you to a gentle and joyful "yes" to Jesus always. "Live by the Spirit and you will certainly not gratify the desire of the flesh."

But when he comes, the Spirit of truth, he will guide you to all truth.
He will not speak on his own, but he will speak what he hears,
and will declare to you the things that are coming.
-John 16:13

Our Guide

You are on a journey with the Body of Christ. Not all things have yet been fully revealed. But God does give you what you need for each day. He will guide you into all His truth, in His time. Come Holy Spirit, teach me.

For you did not receive a spirit of slavery to fall back into fear,
but you received a spirit of adoption, through which we cry, "Abba,
Father!"
-Romans 8:15

Spirit of Adoption

Fear is an enemy that wants to make you cower. But you have been set free by the blood of Jesus. You are adopted into the Family. You can then stand up as His child and cry, "Abba, Father!"

JUNE 15

The Spirit itself bears witness with our spirit that we are children of God,
and if children, then heirs, heirs of God and joint heirs with Christ,
if only we suffer with him so that we may also be glorified with him.
-Romans 8:16-17

Heirs of Heaven

The word suffer comes from the root "to endure."
So you do need to endure with Jesus in order to
be glorified with Him. It's not how God planned
it originally, but thankfully He can use all your
circumstances to bring about His Kingdom, if you
let Him.

JUNE 16

"Whoever loves me will keep my word, and my Father will love him,
and we will come to him and make our dwelling with him."
-John 14:23

Just Obey

Jesus mercifully shows us how to find Him: Keep
His Word. If we just obey, the Father will love us,
and God will come to us and dwell with us, forever.

"The LORD, the LORD, a merciful and gracious God,
slow to anger and rich in kindness and fidelity."
~Exodus 34:6

Slow to Anger

God proclaimed His ineffable name and nature to
Moses. He is merciful. He is gracious. He is slow to
anger and rich, rich in lovingkindness and fidelity.
Call on Him today. That being said, do not take
Him for granted.

~ **JUNE 18** ~

Blessed are you who look into the depths
from your throne upon the cherubim,
praiseworthy and exalted above all forever.
-Daniel 3:55

His Gaze

The eyes of God see far indeed. His gaze penetrates
the depths ... of the earth, and of our hearts as well.
Invite Him to look into your heart, and ask Him
in His mercy to cleanse you of all iniquity and help
you in your weakness, that you might see Him and
live.

Finally, brothers, rejoice. Mend your ways, encourage one another,
agree with one another, live in peace,
and the God of love and peace will be with you.
-2 Corinthians 13:11

Encourage

To encourage literally means "to give heart to."
Share the heart of Jesus beating in you with others,
especially the poor and those on the periphery,
those weighed down in any way. Remember, we're
all on the same journey.

∽ **JUNE 20** ∽

Greet one another with a holy kiss.
-2 Corinthians 13:12

A Kiss

A kiss is an intimate gesture. It doesn't mean you
are perfect or without fault, but it is a sign of your
love for another. Yes we need to work out our
salvation, but even now we can greet one another
with love, His love, His kiss.

The grace of the Lord Jesus Christ and the love of God
and the fellowship of the holy Spirit be with all of you.
-2 Corinthians 13:13

Be Blessed

Today, receive the blessing of God, the Father, Son, and Holy Spirit. The Blessed Trinity looks upon you with favor and grace. You are blessed by the Lord of heaven and earth!

JUNE 22

For God so loved the world that he gave his only Son, so that everyone who
believes in him might not perish but might have eternal life.
-John 3:16

God so loved

For God so loved *you!* God's love shines through your brokenness to surround you with His grace and forgiveness. He pours out His mercy on you like honey. Receive His love like the Prodigal Son received the embrace of his father. Take time today to thank Him.

You must keep his statutes and commandments which I enjoin on you
today, that you and your children after you may prosper,
and that you may have long life on the land which the LORD, your God,
is giving you forever."
-Deuteronomy 4:40

Keep His Statutes

God desires to live in you through your own free assent. Hence, the commandments. If you obey, He promises to bless not only you but your offspring as well, on the land which He is giving you ... forever.

∽ JUNE 24 ∽

The cup of blessing that we bless, is it not a participation in the blood of
Christ? The bread that we break, is it not a participation
in the body of Christ?
-1 Corinthians 10:16

Participation

The Body and Blood of Christ are always new for you, always full of His power and presence, always efficacious in healing you and fortifying you. When you receive Jesus in the Holy Eucharist, you receive Him in His Body and Blood, Soul and Divinity. God has given you all of Himself that you might give all of yourself to Him and others.

How much more will the blood of Christ, who through the eternal spirit
offered himself unblemished to God,
cleanse our consciences from dead works to worship the living God.
-Hebrews 9:14

Cleansed

It is perhaps impossible to overstate that we do not need our "dead works" in order to somehow win God's favor. He has extended His love to us while we were yet sinners, and it remains extended even when we still fail. Let the blood of Jesus cleanse you from all unrighteousness today.

If we love one another, God remains in us,
and his love is brought to perfection in us.
-1 John 4:12

Love On

Love is an act. If you choose to act in love, you will find that God does indeed remain in you, and His love will be brought to completion in you. So, seek to love today.

～⁓ **JUNE 27** ⁓～

"Come to me, all you who labor and are burdened, and I will give you rest."

-Matthew 11:28

Come to Me

In this beloved passage, Jesus reveals Himself as your best Friend. He invites you, now, to come to Him just as you are. Bring Him your troubles; bring Him your cares. Find in Him a place to lay your burdens down, and rest. Today, come to Jesus!

～⁓ **JUNE 28** ⁓～

For this reason I kneel before the Father,
from whom every family in heaven and on earth is named.
-Ephesians 3:14-15

I Kneel

Saint Paul kneels to pray for you before the One from whom your family takes its nature, that God would strengthen you with power through His Spirit in your inner self, that Christ might dwell in your hearts by faith.

They shall look on him whom they have thrust through,
and they shall mourn for him as one mourns for an only son.
-Zechariah 12:10

An Only Son

A day is coming when every eye shall look upon
Jesus and mourn for Him. Now is the time for you
to repent, receive Him, and allow Him to transform
you into His image.

For thus says the Lord GOD: I myself will look after and tend my sheep. As a
shepherd tends his flock when he finds himself among his scattered sheep,
so will I tend my sheep. I will rescue them from every place
where they were scattered when it was cloudy and dark.
-Ezekiel 34:11-12

As a Shepherd

Sheep scatter in times of trouble. Only the Lord
God knows where you're hiding and what you've
suffered. He promises to find you, to rescue you,
and to bring you home to safety.

When he had accomplished purification from sins,
he took his seat at the right hand of the Majesty on high,
as far superior to the angels
as the name he has inherited is more excellent than theirs.
-Hebrews 1:3-4

Higher than the Angels

This Lord who is infinitely superior to the angels has given Himself to you in love. In love, give yourself to Him.

How can I repay the LORD
for all the good done for me?
I will raise the cup of salvation
and call on the name of the LORD.
-Psalm 116:13-14

The Cup of Salvation

What return can you make to the Lord for all He has done for you? He tells you: Receive Him in the Holy Eucharist. Raise up the cup of salvation, and call on the name of the Lord.

For it was fitting that he, for whom and through whom all things exist,
in bringing many children to glory,
should make the leader to their salvation perfect through suffering.
-Hebrews 2:10

Perfect through Suffering

Jesus was made perfect in His humanity through His filial obedience unto death. Through Him, God leads you from glory to glory, as you continue to seek and obey Him.

First of all, then, I ask that supplications, prayers, petitions, and
thanksgivings be offered for everyone, for kings and for all in authority,
that we may lead a quiet and tranquil life in all devotion and dignity.
-1 Timothy 2:1-2

Prayer for Authorities

Peace is the tranquility of order. God wants us to pray for those in authority, that we might live peaceful lives. Pray daily for your public servants, in gratitude, faith and hope.

"My heart exults in the LORD,
my horn is exalted in my God.
I have swallowed up my enemies;
I rejoice in my victory.
-1 Samuel 2:1

Exult in the Lord!

Victories come after battles. If you're struggling physically, spiritually, relationally, financially, or otherwise, praise God in the conflict. The best is yet to come!

∽ JULY 6 ∽

Now since the children share in blood and flesh, he likewise shared in them,
that through death he might ... free those who through fear of death had
been subject to slavery all their life.
-Hebrews 2:14-15

Free from Fear

Jesus died to free you from the cruel tyrant of fear. Are you ready to cast it out of your life? Do you want to be set free? Ask the intercession of Mother Mary and of Saint Michael the Archangel.

JULY 7

Anxiety in a man's heart depresses it,
but a kindly word makes it glad.
-Proverbs 12:25

A Good Word

Worry weighs you down; but a good word lifts you up! Today, ask God to help you encourage someone who could use a boost. The first step is often just your willingness to listen and be fully present to the other.

JULY 8

"Those who are well do not need a physician, but the sick do.
I did not come to call the righteous but sinners."
-Mark 2:17

Sick Call

You can find hope in this promise today. The parts of you that are yet unhealed, broken, and resistant to grace, are the very reason Jesus came. Let Him in. One step at a time, seek to let go and surrender to Him. This Doctor still makes house calls.

∼ JULY 9 ∼

I waited, waited for the LORD;
who bent down and heard my cry.

-Psalm 40:2

I Waited

Sometimes you need to wait, and continue waiting, on the Lord. Be assured that the Master is at work. He will incline His face towards you, and surely hear your cry. This Master Surgeon knows how to gently yet adeptly heal your heart.

∼ JULY 10 ∼

"To you who have been sanctified in Christ Jesus, called to be holy,"

-1 Corinthians 1:2

Holy Love

Christ Jesus has sanctified you. He has made you holy in your spirit. He is transforming you into His image. Now He calls you to live out this grace, by faith that works through love. Do an unexpected act of kindness today!

"He is the one who will baptize with the holy Spirit."

-John 1:33

New Beginnings

Only Jesus has the authority to immerse us in His Spirit and make us new. Carefully prepare yourself for prayer today and ask Him to renew the fire of His Presence in you.

∽ JULY 12 ∽

Avoid immorality. Every other sin a person commits is outside the body, but the immoral person sins against his own body.

-1 Corinthians 6:18

Avoid Immorality

God reveals a sobering truth here. Pray for the grace of chastity. Ask God to create in you a clean heart and to renew in you a steadfast spirit. Ask Him to purify your intentions. Implore the intercession of Saint Joseph. Be free!

They said to him, "Rabbi ... where are you staying?"
-John 1:38

Where Do You Stay?

Jesus encountered people one at a time. He was fully present to them and responded to their hearts. What would you like to ask Jesus today? Then, listen. Prayer, like all good communications, is a two-way street.

∽ JULY 14 ∽

"You have kept the good wine until now."
-John 2:10

Until Now

God often seems to act differently than we expect, sometimes to our chagrin, but always to our benefit. Be on the lookout for unexpected blessings today, and trust God even when things look dim. He will serve the good wine at exactly the right time.

He is able to deal patiently with the ignorant and erring.

-Hebrews 5:2

Patience

These words refer to the high priest of the Old Testament, but they can also describe the attitude of our chief High Priest, Jesus Christ. Remember that you too were anointed as priest, prophet, and king in your Baptism. Jesus has untold patience with you; be patient with yourself and others.

~ JULY 16 ~

For the gifts and the call of God are irrevocable.

-Romans 11:29

A Second Chance

Do you ever feel that God has entrusted to you some spiritual gift —a desire to pray for others, to serve, to counsel, etc.—and you have wasted or misused it? Do not be dismayed, but rise up and exercise it now, for God does not take back His gifts or callings.

Blessed be the LORD, my rock,
who trains my hands for battle,
my fingers for war.
-Psalm 144:1

My Rock

Today, praise God for who He is: Your Rock, Your Fortress, and Your Personal Trainer! He prepares you for victory in the daily battle with the world, the flesh, and the devil. What's more, He always causes you to triumph in Him.

[Jesus] is always able to save those who approach God through him,
since he lives forever to make intercession for them.
-Hebrews 7:25

Savior

This is a most comforting truth. No matter where you're at today, Jesus has you covered! Not only did He give totally of Himself for you on earth, He continues to do so in heaven. Be encouraged, and keep on keeping on. The Son of God Himself is on your side!

And whenever unclean spirits saw him they would fall down before
him and shout, "You are the Son of God."

-Mark 3:11

The Son of God

In case you are ever tempted by the lie that Satan's power is equal to God's, just remember this verse. Speak the name of Jesus today over any problem, any disease, anything that would block His presence in your heart. It is true that He is the Son of Man— but first He is the Son of God!

JULY 20

O LORD of hosts, restore us;
Let your face shine upon us,
that we may be saved.

-Psalm 80:4

Restore Us!

The Lord has restoration ready for you, if you will call on Him today. He wants to radiate His presence on you, if you will just ask. Let Him save and renew you now. Call upon His name and be honest with Him. Then trust in Him, and He will act.

For the yoke that burdened them,
the pole on their shoulder,
And the rod of their taskmaster
you have smashed, as on the day of Midian.
-Isaiah 9:3

Smashed and Shattered

When God does something, He does it completely. He has shattered the yokes, burdens, and rods that you have struggled under. He calls you now to go forward. Make this a beautiful day for someone else. Lift up your head and heart, and receive the mercy of Jesus!

Remember no more the sins of my youth;
remember me only in light of your love.
-Psalm 25:7

Lighten My Load

In truth, the Lord does not remember your sin once it is confessed and forgiven. But *you* may, and He wants to free you of this baggage. Pray Psalm 25 today with a fervent heart.

∼ JULY 23 ∼

"Do not be saddened this day,
for rejoicing in the LORD must be your strength!"
-Nehemiah 8:10

The Joy of the Lord

What an awesome gift God gives us in His joy. Can you imagine His bliss in heaven? Receive His joy today, and let it strengthen you in your spirit, soul, and body. Ask God to give you a new song in your heart and a new spring in your step.

∼ JULY 24 ∼

Indeed, the parts of the body that seem to be weaker
are all the more necessary.
1 Corinthians 12:22

Necessary

Do you ever feel unimportant or overlooked in the Body of Christ? Be encouraged. In your weakness and perceived insignificance you are all the more necessary. God does not see as we see—He sees the heart. Pray that Jesus will increase in you today, and serve with His love.

"He has sent me to proclaim ...
a year acceptable to the Lord."
-Luke 4:18-19

Now

Have you ever wondered when is the right time to act in or for the Lord? Jesus answers the question. Now is an acceptable time; today is the day of salvation. Ask God to direct your paths today, to lead you in His ways, for *His* sake.

∽ JULY 26 ∽

Christ, offered once to take away the sins of many,
will appear a second time, not to take away sin but to bring salvation
to those who eagerly await him.
-Hebrews 9:28

Longing

To know Jesus is to know longing, because He is so beautiful, so wonderful, yet sometimes so hidden. Even so, He will return to bring the fullness of salvation to you as you eagerly anticipate it. Remain fervent in your heart and wait expectantly for Him.

Therefore, do not throw away your confidence;
it will have great recompense. You need endurance to do the will of
God and receive what he has promised.
-Hebrews 10:35-36

Hold On!

This is a rich promise! Your faith, tested and tried as it may be, will have a great reward. So, DO NOT throw it away in a time of trouble or temptation! But hold on for greater things. "No ear has ever heard, no eye seen, any God but you doing such deeds for those who wait for him" (Isaiah 64:4).

I will place my law within them, and write it upon their hearts;
I will be their God, and they shall be my people.
-Jeremiah 31:33

Written On Our Hearts

As children, we had educators instruct us about truth. However, God promises to actually *inscribe* His truth upon our hearts. Give Him a *tabula rasa* —an empty slate—on which to write. Rejoice in this amazing assurance!

"'I will fix a place for my people Israel;
I will plant them so that they may
dwell in their place without further disturbance.'"
-2 Samuel 7:10

Fixed

God honors His Word to Israel, His chosen people forever. Similarly, He will honor His Word to you. It may not be fully accomplished yet, but be of good cheer. He has overcome the world, and He will establish you so that you may live in righteousness and peace.

And some seed fell on rich soil and produced fruit.
It came up and grew and yielded thirty, sixty, and a hundredfold.
-Mark 4:8

Yield

Jesus has sowed good seed on the many paths of your life. Let today be the day that His Word finds a deep, rich soil in your heart. Spend time today in the Scripture. Let God's Word sink deep into your spirit, and grow to produce a great harvest!

We must consider how to rouse one another to love and good works.
-Hebrews 10:24

Wake Up!

There is no such thing as a Lone Ranger in the Body of Christ. God has created us in such a way that we need one another, and that's a very good thing! Today, reflect on ways to move your brothers and sisters to acts of love and service.

We should not stay away from our assembly,
as is the custom of some, but encourage one another,
and this all the more as you see the day drawing near.
-Hebrews 10:25

Stay Connected

God calls us to gather for regular worship. The idea of an exclusive "personal worship experience" that omits others is not from God, for God is love, and true love goes out to others; it is self-donating.

But I will leave as a remnant in your midst
a people humble and lowly,
Who shall take refuge in the name of the LORD.
-Zephaniah 3:12

A Remnant

The Lord looks for those who want Him to be their all in all. You can be that person today by your trust and surrender. You are part of a faithful remnant. So be faithful, and remain!

∽ AUGUST 3 ∽

"Blessed are they who mourn,
for they will be comforted."
-Matthew 5:4

Mourning Glory

It's hard to be hopeful when you're heartbroken. Still, Jesus calls you to look to Him. You are not alone. As you turn to Him, receive His promise of comfort today. Jesus offers you more than just a sense of well-being. He wants to work through your sorrows and turn them into joy.

For it is I this day
who have made you a fortified city.
-Jeremiah 1:18

Fortified

Only the Lord can make you into His spokesperson for the world. It is He who strengthens you to be who He is calling you to be, to fulfill your destiny, to do His will. Therefore, spend time today getting closer to your heavenly Father. Ask Him to reveal Himself. He will.

As I watched,
Thrones were set up
and the Ancient One took his throne.
His clothing was snow bright,
and the hair on his head as white as wool;
His throne was flames of fire,
with wheels of burning fire.
-Daniel 7:9

Ruler

All heaven is silent as the Ancient One approaches His Throne. The God who created you and loves you, the God whom you serve, reigns supreme. Today, worship Him. If possible, go to Mass and enter into the heavenly liturgy.

"This is my beloved Son, with whom I am well pleased; listen to him."
-Matthew 17:5

My Beloved

God affirms Jesus on the Mount of Transfiguration in a most glorious and striking manner. He has a directive for us as well: "Listen to Him." Indeed. Take some time today to do just that!

∽ AUGUST 7 ∾

For I handed on to you as of first importance what I also received:
that Christ died for our sins in accordance with the scriptures.
-1 Corinthians 15:3

Primary Importance

Jesus lived to die for you. He gave Himself for your salvation from sin. He knew there was no other way for you to be saved—from eternal death, from sin and its consequences. Let this continue to be a life-changing truth for you. You matter to Him immensely!

Do not be afraid any longer, little flock,
for your Father is pleased to give you the kingdom.
-Luke 12:32

His Pleasure

What a wonderful command from our Lord:
"Don't fear any longer. Enough already. Your
Father is pleased to give you the kingdom." This is
an astounding announcement. Receive this promise
in humble gratitude today, and walk tall.

"Gird your loins and light your lamps and be like servants who await their
master's return from a wedding, ready to open immediately
when he comes and knocks."
-Luke 12:35-36

Light Your Lamp

The clarion call has been sounded. It's time to get
ready and stay steady. Ask God to reveal His will for
your life to you. Ask Him to show you how to be
prepared for Him. Gird your loins with the belt of
truth and light your lamps with the fire of the Holy
Spirit. Be ready to open instantly, at the sound of
the first knock!

I thank you, LORD, with all my heart;
before the gods to you I sing. ...
When I cried out, you answered;
you strengthened my spirit.
-Psalm 138:1; 3

Thank You Lord!

God is with you to deliver you from all your difficulties today. Trust in Him; call on Him. He will deliver you and glorify you, and grant you *His* salvation.

∽ **AUGUST 11** ∼

"Amen, I say to you, no prophet is accepted in his own native place."
-Luke 4:24

Recognition

While this Scriptural truth can be difficult to hear, it can also be a reminder that God calls you to look only to Himself for your affirmation and approval.

"So you too must befriend the alien,
for you were once aliens yourselves in the land of Egypt."
-Deuteronomy 10:19

No Longer Strangers

We are called to be merciful; we must show mercy
to others—especially those whom, as Pope Francis
says, live on the physical, financial, and relational
peripheries of life. And the wonderful paradox is,
that as we do so, we receive mercy ourselves. We
"get in the way" of grace.

∽ **AUGUST 13** ∽

Jesus said to them, "The Son of Man is to be handed over to men,
and they will kill him, and he will be raised on the third day."
-Matthew 17:22-23

A Hard Word

It is hard to hear difficult news. But our Heavenly
Father has you always in His provident care. If
He does call you to endure hardship, He will
nonetheless give you all you need to bear it. Today,
pray for those who are persecuted for righteousness'
sake, throughout the world.

"It is the LORD who marches before you; he will be with you and will
never fail you or forsake you. So do not fear or be dismayed."

-Deuteronomy 31:8

Follow Fearlessly

Over and over again the Lord tells you, "I will be
with you. Be not afraid. I will never forsake you."
Today, reflect on this promise until you feel His
strength well up within you. Then act as He leads.

∽∾ **AUGUST 15** ∽∾

A great sign appeared in the sky, a woman clothed with the sun,
with the moon under her feet, and on her head a crown of twelve stars.

-Revelation 12:1

A Great Sign

Mary, Mother of the Messiah, is a symbol of
the Church in her struggle against the "ancient
serpent." You live in a battle, but the battle belongs
to the Lord. Today, ask your spiritual Mother to
pray with you and for you unto the Lord.

Therefore, do not continue in ignorance,
but try to understand what is the will of the Lord.
-Ephesians 5:17

Seek to Know

Do not allow yourself to be seduced by distraction
or lulled by lies, but try to discern and comprehend
what God is telling you. He has the plan; ask those
wiser than you to help you decipher it. As you obey,
clearer will be the way.

∽∾ **AUGUST 17** ∽∾

Let us rid ourselves of every burden and sin that clings to us and persevere
in running the race that lies before us while keeping our eyes fixed on Jesus,
the leader and perfecter of faith
-Hebrews 12:1-2

Run!

You have a race to run, a crown to win, and
an inheritance to possess. Run this race with
endurance, looking to Jesus, Jesus, only Jesus. He
will encourage you, run with you, and even run in
you! Turn from sin, and run with Him.

Do you think that I have come to establish peace on the earth?
No, I tell you, but rather division.
-Luke 12:51

Division

Jesus is Lord. Alone. You cannot serve two masters.
Because He loves you so much, He will continually
purify you and divide you from lesser loves, that you
might love Him with your whole heart.

∾ AUGUST 19 ∾

"It is easier for a camel to pass through the eye of a needle
than for one who is rich to enter the kingdom of God."
Matthew 19:24

Let It Go

Only God can divest you of your attachment to
your possessions. The question is, will you let Him?
Are you willing to surrender your ownership and
control to Him? Are you willing to rely only on
Him? Today, give something away.

"Thus, the last will be first, and the first will be last."
-Matthew 20:16

Stay Low

Let's face it. It's hard to remain always yielded to God. Can't you keep just a little bit for yourself? As usual, Jesus doesn't mince words. Stay low; stay humble; stay His.

∽ AUGUST 21 ∽

At the time, all discipline seems a cause not for joy but for pain, yet later it brings the peaceful fruit of righteousness to those who are trained by it.
-Hebrews 12:11

His

This verse speaks for itself. The good news is that God holds you in His loving hands even in your trials. Be encouraged today. You are God's own. He is preparing you for greater things.

Let them praise his name in festive dance,
make music with tambourine and lyre.
For the LORD takes delight in his people,
honors the poor with victory.

-Psalm 149:3-4

The Lord's Delight

The Lord takes delight in you! Isn't that awesome?
You are the light of His eyes. Praise Him! Kick up
your heels! He will honor you with victory today.

∼ **AUGUST 23** ∼

"Woe to you, scribes and Pharisees, you hypocrites. You lock the kingdom of
heaven before human beings. You do not enter yourselves,
nor do you allow entrance to those trying to enter."

-Matthew 23:13

Enter In!

Woe indeed, to those who would try to hinder you
from receiving the kingdom Jesus died to give you.
Believe that God earnestly desires a relationship
with you. Receive the sacraments of the Eucharist
and Reconciliation more frequently, and enter in!

Nathanael said to him, "Can anything good come from Nazareth?"
Philip said to him, "Come and see."
-John 1:46

Anything Good?

Nazareth sounds like a "wrong side of the tracks" place. Yet Philip persists in his invitation and Nathaniel—Bartholomew—meets the Messiah. Be open to the Spirit today! Also, be persistent. The enemy wants us to cave in, while Jesus wants and expects us to complete His Will.

∽∾ AUGUST 25 ∽∾

For this reason we too give thanks to God unceasingly, that, in receiving the
word of God from hearing us, you received not a human word but,
as it truly is, the word of God, which is now at work in you who believe.
-1 Thessalonians 2:13

The Word of Power

Truly the Word of God, flowing from His Holy Spirit, contains power in itself to change you, transform you, and bring you to life. Believe this truth. Ask the Holy Spirit to ignite His Word within you in a new way. Come Holy Spirit!

God is faithful, and by him you were called to fellowship with his Son,
Jesus Christ our Lord.
-1 Corinthians 1:9

Called

It's good to remember who initiated this whole adventure of faith ... none other than God Himself! He called you, He invited you to fellowship with Jesus. And He awaits your RSVP!

∽ **AUGUST 27** ∽
Light dawns for the just;
gladness, for the honest of heart.
Rejoice in the LORD, you just,
and praise his holy name.
-Psalm 97:11-12

Dawn

Light will dawn for you, and joy will gladden your heart. The dawn comes gradually, but the day arrives in glory! Continue to trust in the Lord; continue to walk in His way. He will never forsake you.

Water quenches a flaming fire,
and alms atone for sins.
-Sirach 3:29

Doused

Sin has consequences in us and around us; but so does godly obedience and mercy. Today, give alms; open your heart and give cheerfully. Thus will the fire be quenched, and you will feel His joy.

꧁ AUGUST 29 ꧂

"When you hold a banquet, invite the poor, the crippled, the lame, the blind; blessed indeed will you be because of their inability to repay you. For you will be repaid at the resurrection of the righteous."
-Luke 14:13-14

Be a Friend

Try something new today. Give a blessing to someone who is unable to repay you. If possible, do it secretly. You may be surprised at your reward.

∞ **AUGUST 30** ∞

I resolved to know nothing while I was with you except Jesus Christ,
and him crucified.

-1 Corinthians 2:2

Only Jesus

It can be so tempting to show off your real or "imagined" knowledge, and so humbling to simply be authentic. Yet note the choice of the world's greatest evangelist.

∞ **AUGUST 31** ∞

The LORD is my light and my salvation;
whom do I fear?
The LORD is my life's refuge;
of whom am I afraid?

-Psalm 27:1

The Lord Is My Light!

Say this verse out loud. It is so powerful. You are not alone. God is with you always. There is nothing to fear. Receive Your refuge and strength. In spiritual communion, receive Jesus now.

*We have not received the spirit of the world but the Spirit that is from God,
so that we may understand the things freely given us by God.*

-1 Corinthians 2:12

Deeper Insight

God liberally gives us His Spirit and the things of His Spirit, "things into which the angels longed to look" (1 Peter 1:12). Therefore, let us seek the Lord more diligently. Let us seek to know Him better and to better understand the things of the Spirit.

∽ **SEPTEMBER 2** ∽

*Jesus said to Simon, "Do not be afraid;
from now on you will be catching men."*

-Luke 5:10

A Catch from the Deep

God had prepared a great school of fish for Peter, but Peter still had to catch them. Similarly, God has prepared hearts to receive Him—ask Him to bring the catch to you.

Persevere in the faith, firmly grounded, stable,
and not shifting from the hope of the gospel that you heard.

-Colossians 1:23

Grounded

Faith is your most precious gift from on high. Yet you must persist in it, reading and reflecting on God's Word, worshipping at Mass, receiving the sacraments, growing in love, grounded in your heavenly hope.

"The Son of Man is lord of the sabbath."

-Luke 6:5

Good Sabbath!

God gave us the Sabbath as a day of rest, worship, and family. True leisure is to taste the good, to know the true, and to see the beautiful. Let Him be Lord of your Lord's Day! Especially take time to be alone with Him. It pleases God when you, His child, enjoy His presence and His faithful love.

Did not God choose those who are poor in the world to be rich in faith and heirs of the kingdom that he promised to those who love him?

-James 2:5

Poor yet Rich

Poverty is not a blessing per se, yet it is a perennial truth that those with less tend to rely more on God. Today, reckon yourself as poor and even detached from your possessions that you might become rich in faith.

My soul, be at rest in God alone,
from whom comes my hope.

-Psalm 62:6

Rest in Him Alone

Today, receive the rest of God. Find a quiet place and just allow His peace to pour over you like honey. You are not your own. You have been bought with a price that is in every way out of this world. Let His hope become yours now.

Do you not know that the unjust will not inherit the kingdom of God?

-1 Corinthians 6:9

Sobriety

This is a sobering truth. We are not to judge persons but we must judge behavior, beginning with our own. Only holiness can inherit holiness. He is no fool who gives away what he cannot keep to gain that which he cannot lose.

"Behold, the virgin shall be with child and bear a son,
and they shall name him Emmanuel,"
which means "God is with us."

-Matthew 1:23

Virgin

And the virgin's name was Mary. Mary indeed acquiesced to the Father's will and plan, looking always to God, and always after her Son. Look to her, the Star of the Sea, to guide you always, and call on her to lead you to Jesus. God gave Mary a most unique and grace-filled vocation; He has given you one as well.

Be merciful, just as [also] your Father is merciful.

-Luke 6:36

Mercy

First, receive God's mercy. Be merciful to yourself. Forgive yourself. Believe that you matter to God, because you do. Then reach out. Act. Move. Take an action out of love. Do something simple and good for another.

Do you not know that the runners in the stadium all run in the race, but only one wins the prize? Run so as to win.

-1 Corinthians 9:24

Run to Win!

You have a race to run, a prize to win ... but in this stadium, your victory brings glory to God and good to all men. Therefore, let go of whatever weighs you down or slows you up. Run to win!

Indeed, the grace of our Lord has been abundant,
along with the faith and love that are in Christ Jesus.
-1 Timothy 1:14

Get In the Way of Grace

God is an abundant, generous Father. Why then do you sometimes feel dry and weak? Take time with Him; then act on His Word. As you serve, grace will be multiplied *to* you and *through* you for others.

∽ SEPTEMBER 12 ∽

"'Rejoice with me because I have found my lost sheep.'"
-Luke 15:6

Celebrate!

Rejoice with the Lord who rejoices in you today. He is restoring your heart even as you read this. The path is difficult and it's easy to get lost. Abide with Jesus today. Let Him lead you back to the fold.

Moreover, they should be tested first; then,
if there is nothing against them, let them serve as deacons.
-1 Timothy 3:10

Examine

It is typically easier to rule than to serve, which is why those who would serve must first be tested. As Pope Francis says, it is good for a shepherd to smell like his sheep.

∽∾ **SEPTEMBER 14** ∽∾

May I never boast except in the cross of our Lord Jesus Christ,
through which the world has been crucified to me, and I to the world.
-Galatians 6:14

No Boast

Only in Jesus and His Cross can you find understanding, compassion, vision, and virtue. Thus may you never boast except in this Cross, which lifts you and the world up to the Father.

"(And you yourself a sword will pierce) so that the
thoughts of many hearts may be revealed."
-Luke 2:34-35

Pierced

At Calvary, the prophesied sword of sorrow did
indeed pierce Mary's heart, leaving a laceration
through which the wounds of your heart can now
be both revealed and healed. Receive what Our
Lord did for you. Surrender to Him and ask Him to
heal you. Mary will help you.

Rejoice, you just, in the LORD;
praise from the upright is fitting.
Give thanks to the LORD on the harp;
on the ten-stringed lyre offer praise.
-Psalm 33:1-2

Praise!

At times it's good to just take a few moments and
spontaneously worship the Lord in song. If you play
an instrument, so much the better! Praise Him with
joy! "Let the faithful rejoice in their glory, cry out
for joy at their banquet, With the praise of God in
their mouth." (Psalm 149:5-6).

Attend to yourself and to your teaching; persevere in both tasks,
for by doing so you will save both yourself and those who listen to you.
-1 Timothy 4:16

Attention!

Pope Francis teaches that each of us is "a mission on this earth," called to illuminate, bless, enliven, and heal. Pay attention to your soul and your call, for the rewards are eternal. If you're unsure about either, consider asking a priest or spiritual counselor for discernment and direction.

The person who is trustworthy in very small matters is also trustworthy in
great ones; and the person who is dishonest in very small matters
is also dishonest in great ones.
-Luke 16:10

Worthy of Trust

Jesus refers here specifically to our use of wealth. Do you use the goods of this earth wisely and with a care for others, or are you untruthful and self-seeking only? If the latter, then stop. You are on the wrong path. Ask God to give you a generous heart.

"Take care, then, how you hear. To anyone who has, more will be given,
and from the one who has not,
even what he seems to have will be taken away."
-Luke 8:18

More or Less

There is a risk in just hearing the Word of God without applying it. It might appear that you have as much as others, but only as you use it shall you be given more. So, obey God and move out in His work!

To do what is right and just
is more acceptable to the LORD than sacrifice.
-Proverbs 21:3

Decision

When you sometimes feel unsure about what to do, quiet down and ask the Lord, "What is my next best move?" Listen attentively to His answer. Then act. He is pleased with your obedience.

As Jesus passed on from there, he saw a man named Matthew sitting at the
customs post. He said to him, "Follow me."
And he got up and followed him.
-Matthew 9:9

Chosen

This is the passage referred to by Pope Francis in his papal motto: *Miserando sed Eligendo.* Jesus looked at Mathew with compassion, and said, "Follow Me." Today He looks at you with love. "I choose you," He says. How will you respond?

Sing and rejoice, O daughter Zion!
See, I am coming to dwell among you, says the LORD.
-Zechariah 2:14

He Is Coming

God doesn't make promises that He can't keep. He has chosen Zion, and He will dwell among them. Even so, He now dwells among us, and in us, by the power of His Holy Spirit, the "down payment" for those who believe. The Presence of God, once enthroned between the Cherubim in the Ark of the Covenant, now abides in *your* spirit!

Confess your sins to one another and pray for one another, that you may be healed. The fervent prayer of a righteous person is very powerful.

-James 5:16

Fervent Prayer

When we confess, we agree with God that we have missed the mark. Receive the sacrament of Reconciliation often and pray earnestly for others. Your heartfelt prayer will bring the fire of heaven to earth, and the presence of God to others.

∽ **SEPTEMBER 24** ∽

Lord, you have been our refuge through all generations. ...
But humans you return to dust,
saying, "Return, you mortals!"
-Psalm 90:1, 3

Our Refuge

God is your refuge always, especially in light of the inevitable reality of death. Today, take time to consciously put your trust in Him, and come to know His peace.

SEPTEMBER 25

Woe to the complacent in Zion,
to the overconfident on the mount of Samaria,
Leaders of a nation favored from the first,
to whom the people of Israel have recourse!
-Amos 6:1

Woe!

It can happen so easily. God blesses us; we grow accustomed to it; we start taking Him for granted. But Jesus never did that. He rose early morning to spend time alone with His Father. Let us look to Him and do the same.

SEPTEMBER 26

Thus says the LORD of hosts:
I am intensely jealous for Zion,
stirred to jealous wrath for her.
-Zechariah 8:1-2

Jealous for You

God is not only jealous, he is *intensely* jealous for His people, which includes you! You matter to Him! He desires you! Tell Him you love Him today. Seek the Lord, while He may be found.

Let them thank the LORD for such kindness,
such wondrous deeds for mere mortals.
For he satisfied the thirsty,
filled the hungry with good things.
-Psalm 107:8-9

Give!

God is a wonderful, abundant, creative giver! But He didn't create you to just be an observer. No, He calls you into the action. Today, give of yourself to someone else. Feed those who hunger, both physically and otherwise; give drink to those who thirst.

"Whoever is not against you is for you."
-Luke 9:50

Allow

The apostles were upset because someone outside their "group" was doing good in Jesus' name. Have you ever felt that way? Jesus teaches us that God is moving in many ways in many different people; let us seek to encourage the good and resist the evil.

God commands the angels
to guard you in all your ways.
With their hands they shall support you,
lest you strike your foot against a stone.
-Psalm 91:11-12

His Angels

Just think, you always have angels watching over you! They keep you safe, they guide your ways, and they support your steps. They are God's messengers for you. Today, thank your Guardian Angel.

Indeed, the word of God is living and effective,
sharper than any two-edged sword,
penetrating even between soul and spirit, joints and marrow,
and able to discern reflections and thoughts of the heart.
-Hebrews 4:12

His Word

God's Word was never meant to gather dust on a shelf. It's ALIVE! Today, open the Bible and let God's Word move your heart and hands. Ask the Holy Spirit to anoint His Word, to make it real for you.

He found them in a wilderness,
a wasteland of howling desert.
He shielded them and cared for them,
guarding them as the apple of his eye.
-Deuteronomy 32:10

The Apple of His Eye

As He found Israel, so the Lord finds you in the wilderness and in the wastelands of your life. He longs to shield and care for you. Return His love today. Be the apple of His eye!

∾ OCTOBER 2 ∾

"See that you do not despise one of these little ones, for I say to you that
their angels in heaven always look upon the face of my heavenly Father."
-Matthew 18:10

The Little Ones

Do not make the mistake of looking down on children, or on the unnoticed, simple people of the earth, for their mighty angels, along with the seraphim and cherubim, always gaze with love on the Face of the Most High.

Have no anxiety at all, but in everything, by prayer and petition,
with thanksgiving, make your requests known to God.
Then the peace of God that surpasses all understanding
will guard your hearts and minds in Christ Jesus.
-Philippians 4:6-7

No Fear

Here is the secret to peace. Tell God your requests, your needs, and thank Him in advance for the answers. Then leave everything to Him. When anxieties arise, surrender again. His peace will guard your heart.

"Blessed are the poor in spirit,
for theirs is the kingdom of heaven."
-Matthew 5:3

Poor in Spirit

Blessed are you when you divest yourself of your excess, and live simply. But even if you're not there yet, you can divest yourself of your busyness, and dwell in silent love before your crucified Savior. Blessed will you be, for He wants to give you Himself —the Kingdom of heaven.

"When the Son of Man comes, will he find faith on earth?"

-Luke 18:8

A Sobering Question

You can be part of the answer to this question posed by Jesus if you choose. He's looking for those who will pray with faith, with His Spirit in their hearts, as they wait upon the Lord. He's looking for those who refuse to give in to evil, or give up to sin. Will Jesus find faith...in you?

∽ OCTOBER 6 ∽

When one finds a worthy wife,
her value is far beyond pearls.
Her husband, entrusting his heart to her,
has an unfailing prize.
-Proverbs 31:10-11

An Unfailing Prize

Life can be long, and love must endure much. But it can truly be a joy for you if you choose to entrust your heart and donate yourself to those you love. Today, do an unexpected kindness for your spouse or loved one.

*In the sixth month, the angel Gabriel was sent from God to a town of
Galilee called Nazareth, to a virgin betrothed to a man named Joseph,
of the house of David, and the virgin's name was Mary.*
-Luke 1:26-27

Virgin and Mother

Mary is our Mother. What a relief! God has given
us His very best—again—to help us on our journey
of love. Jesus wanted you to feel what He felt in
His home at Nazareth, so He gave you His mother.
Today pray the Rosary, and thank God for the
Virgin Mary.

"Therefore what God has joined together, no human being must separate."
-Mark 10:9

United in Him

What God has joined together, He is able to keep
together, if we cooperate with Him. Today, pray for
all marriages, for the grace to make Jesus the center
of every union. Ask God to turn the water of daily
life into the wine of ardent love.

On that day it will be said:
"Behold our God, to whom we looked to save us!
This is the LORD for whom we looked;
let us rejoice and be glad that he has saved us!"
-Isaiah 25:9

Behold Our God!

Always and everywhere you need the salvation of God. Like children who can play happily because they know they are safe, you need your Father. Take heart today, for you shall surely behold Him.

"Stand up and go; your faith has saved you."
Luke 17:19

Your Faith

You are not in control. Most of what happens around you is out of your hands. But you can believe, and act on that belief. Today, reach out to God in faith. Your faith, a gift from Him, will save you.

∽ OCTOBER 11 ∽

For freedom Christ set us free; so stand firm
and do not submit again to the yoke of slavery.
-Galatians 5:1

Freedom

Freedom is one of the most fervent desires in the human heart, because God has created us in His image and likeness, and He is absolutely free. Jesus has won this gift for us and imparts it abundantly. Today, stand strong; do not give in to the deceit of sin.

∽ OCTOBER 12 ∽

But as to what is within, give alms, and behold,
everything will be clean for you.
-Luke 11:41

Be Generous

It is a spiritual law that as we give, we are blessed, and even cleansed. Today, pray for the opportunity to give, and then act on it when it comes. Behold, all will be clean for you.

OCTOBER 13

*Those who belong to Christ [Jesus] have crucified their flesh
with its passions and desires.*
-Galatians 5:24

Crucified

You can try to resist temptation on your own, by a sort of white-knuckled approach, but that does not bear fruit. Instead, join your passions and cravings to the Cross of Jesus and ask Him to deliver you from death to life. When temptation comes, surrender your flesh to God and ask Jesus to give you His victory.

OCTOBER 14

*Out of the depths I call to you,
LORD; Lord, hear my cry!
May your ears be attentive
to my cry for mercy.*
-Psalm 130:1-2

From the Depths

Did you know that God is listening for your voice today? Call on Him from the depths of your heart. He can hear you even from rock bottom. Ask Him to pour His mercy over you like rich oil.

I am the vine, you are the branches. Whoever remains in me and I in him
will bear much fruit, because without me you can do nothing.
-John 15:5

Our Source

The secret to life is to abide in Jesus, to long for Him, to hunger for His Word. Take time after you receive Holy Communion to just rest in His loving embrace. There is so much He wants to reveal to you, in His own time and in His own way. But you have to remain on the vine.

He has made known to us the mystery of his will in accord with his favor
that he set forth in him as a plan for the fullness of times,
to sum up all things in Christ, in heaven and on earth.
-Ephesians 1:9-10

His Time

In His own time, God is gathering up all things in Christ Jesus. So when you feel disconnected or distracted, trust in Jesus and be at peace. There's a bigger plan unfolding!

"When they take you before synagogues and before rulers and authorities, do not worry about how or what your defense will be or about what you are to say. For the holy Spirit will teach you at that moment what you should say."

-Luke 12:11-12

No Worries

God promises that He will not only protect us from all our adversaries, He will also give us what to say in our defense. That also means what *not* to say. Trust Him today.

I raise my eyes toward the mountains.
From where will my help come?
My help comes from the LORD,
the maker of heaven and earth.

-Psalm 121:1-2

I Will Lift Up Mine Eyes

God is with you every step of your way. Many times you may need to rest and lift your eyes unto the hills. Do so with hope, and pray the words of this Psalm to the Father who cares for you. "God will not allow your foot to slip; your guardian does not sleep" (Psalm 121:3).

154

For by grace you have been saved through faith, and this is not from you; it
is the gift of God; it is not from works, so no one may boast.

-Ephesians 2:8-9

By Grace

It is by grace, the free gift of God, that you have been saved. As you receive this gift and believe in Jesus, let your boast be in Him. This actually is also a relief. It's not about you! You can get out of yourself and into Christ. Hurrah!

For we are his handiwork, created in Christ Jesus for the good works that
God has prepared in advance, that we should live in them.

-Ephesians 2:10

His Works

This verse is corollary to the previous. You are God's workmanship, created for good works He has ready for you that you should walk in them, and live. May this truly bring you joy today. You are part of an eternal story, which is being written even as you allow God to work through you.

Blessed are those servants whom the master finds vigilant on his arrival.
Amen, I say to you, he will gird himself, have them recline at table,
and proceed to wait on them.
-Luke 12:37

Ready

God wants you to be all in. He wants you to be madly in love with Him, so that when He returns—like a thief in the night—you'll be right where He wants you to be, doing what He wants you to do.

With joy you will draw water
at the fountain of salvation.
-Isaiah 12:3

Drink Up!

The thirstier you are, the better the beverage tastes, right? God promises that you will draw water from the everlasting spring of life with joy. Jesus promises, "Whoever believes in me, as scripture says: 'Rivers of living water will flow from within him'" (John 7:38). Take a drink today!

I, then, a prisoner for the Lord, urge you to live in a manner worthy of the
call you have received, with all humility and gentleness, with patience,
bearing with one another through love.

-Ephesians 4:1-2

Love On!

Your life is not your own. You belong to Jesus, as He has put His Spirit in you and called you to holiness. Therefore, bear with those God has given you, through love. No one less than Saint Paul himself urges you to live worthy of your calling. Today, bear with those God has put in your life, through love.

∽ OCTOBER 24 ∽

"But the tax collector stood off at a distance and would not even raise his
eyes to heaven but beat his breast and prayed,
'O God, be merciful to me a sinner.'"

-Luke 18:13

From a Distance

Jesus, your true Lover, is more concerned with you getting in touch with your true self than parading your virtues. It really is your heart that always seems to need connecting, isn't it? When you feel far away, lead with your weakness.

Be sure of this, that no immoral or impure or greedy person, that is, an
idolater, has any inheritance in the kingdom of Christ and of God.
-Ephesians 5:5

Zero Tolerance

There is simply no place for impurity of any sort
among believers. Instead, be thankful always for the
presence of the Holy God in your life and the Holy
Spirit in your heart.

∽ **OCTOBER 26** ∽

"This daughter of Abraham, whom Satan has bound for eighteen years
now, ought she not to have been set free on the sabbath day
from this bondage?"
-Luke 13:16

Unbound!

Jesus is passionate about your freedom. He wants
to liberate you not only from physical bondage but
from religious misunderstanding as well. Ask Him
to set you free, and spend the Sabbath with Him.

Be subordinate to one another out of reverence for Christ.

-Ephesians 5:21

Defer

Not easy, this one. It takes prudence and humility. Even so, Saint Paul says to do it for Jesus' sake. If He could suffer for me, can I not surrender for Him?

∽ **OCTOBER 28** ∽

Happy are all who fear the LORD,
who walk in the ways of God.
What your hands provide you will enjoy;
you will be happy and prosper.

-Psalm 128:1 2

Blessed

When we reverence God, He rewards us not just in the hereafter, but already here on earth. More than material goods, however, are the peace and love we enjoy from His gentle heart. Praise God!

For I am convinced that neither death, nor life, nor angels,
nor principalities, nor present things, nor future things, nor powers,
nor height, nor depth, nor any other creature will be able to separate us
from the love of God in Christ Jesus our Lord.

-Romans 8:38-39

Covered

Nothing will be able to keep you from God's love. If you are feeling abandoned by the Lord or in dire straits, receive this promise now. God cannot lie. He will deliver you.

Put on the armor of God so that you may be able to stand firm
against the tactics of the devil.

-Ephesians 6:11

Stand!

You have an enemy. Forewarned is forearmed. Memorize Ephesians 6:14-17 and pray it daily for yourself and those in your charge. Ask Jesus to cover you with His Precious Blood. That way you will stand firm and victorious against all attacks of the devil.

They tie up heavy burdens [hard to carry] and lay them on people's
shoulders, but they will not lift a finger to move them.
-Matthew 23:4

Engaged

How are you like a Pharisee? Do you dole out
directives and tasks, whether for family or those in
your charge, and then step aside? Or do you pitch
in and help? Actions speak louder than words.

~ NOVEMBER 1 ~

Blessed are they who hunger and thirst for righteousness,
for they will be satisfied.
-Matthew 5:6

Hungry

We are made for greater things. God has put a
hunger in our hearts for the true, the good, and
the beautiful. To be holy is to love Him and serve
others. Ask God to help you love Jesus more today
than you did yesterday. You will be satisfied.

The souls of the just are in the hand of God,
and no torment shall touch them.

-Wisdom of Solomon 3:1

In His Hands

God has delivered our souls, in Jesus, from the pangs of eternal death. Even though we may suffer as we await the fullness of union with Him, it is in joy and expectation. In this way, we glorify God, who has already won the definitive victory, through His Son, our Lord Jesus Christ.

"Hear, O Israel! The LORD is our God, the LORD alone! Therefore, you
shall love the LORD, your God, with all your heart, and with all your soul,
and with all your strength."

-Deuteronomy 6:4-5

Shema Israel!

God is all and wants to be your all. You are free to respond as you wish to His gracious invitation. Even so, His Word calls you to love Him with your whole self. Jesus gave all of Himself for you; will you do any less?

I have stilled my soul,
hushed it like a weaned child.
Like a weaned child on its mother's lap,
so is my soul within me.

-Psalm 131:2

Hushed

A still soul is like the calm of a deep blue sea: both are serene treasures, especially during the storms of life. Today, take some time with Jesus. Allow Him to quiet and compose your heart.

Have the same regard for one another;
do not be haughty but associate with the lowly.

-Romans 12:16

Lowly

Anawim is a Hebrew word meaning, "the poor who depend on the Lord for deliverance." Saint Paul directs you do your best to love freely each person you encounter, especially fellow believers. Seek out the lowly, the ordinary, simple people—the *anawim*—beloved by the Father.

Finally, brothers, pray for us, so that the word of the Lord may speed forward and be glorified, as it did among you, and that we may be delivered from perverse and wicked people, for not all have faith.

-2 Thessalonians 3:1-2

Into the Breach!

We need to pray that God's Word may move forward through those who share the Gospel by word and deed. You are also called to spread the Word. Godspeed!

For the grace of God has appeared, saving all and training us to reject godless ways and worldly desires and to live temperately, justly, and devoutly in this age.

-Titus 2:11-12

Our Trainer

God's grace has indeed saved you, and trains you to throw away what is impure or selfish and instead to live with equanimity and a fervent heart. As with any training, this takes time, patience, and perseverance. Today, begin again with hope. "For our salvation is nearer now than when we first believed" (Romans 13:11).

And passing into holy souls from age to age,
she produces friends of God and prophets.
-Wisdom of Solomon 7:27

Wisdom

Solomon personifies Wisdom as a splendor of light which passes into those who willingly desire to love God and learn His ways. Do you want to be God's friend? Seek Wisdom.

∾∾ NOVEMBER 9 ∾∾

"For behold, the kingdom of God is among you."
-Luke 17:21

The Kingdom

The Kingdom of God is Jesus Himself. In Him, God is present among us, in many ways, but especially within us, in our hearts. It is the condition where Jesus is Lord. God desires that His Kingdom dwell among us and within us. Wherever you are, in your sphere of influence, you have the opportunity of expanding the presence of Christ Jesus. Today, ask God to grow His Kingdom in you.

For this is love, that we walk according to his commandments; this is the commandment, as you heard from the beginning, in which you should walk.

-2 John 6

This Is Love

In his Letter to us, Saint John is so pure, so transparent. This is how we love God—by walking as He directs us, by reaching out in love to others, by trusting in Jesus. As of old, walk this way.

Whoever seeks to preserve his life will lose it,
but whoever loses it will save it.

-Luke 17:33

Let Go

The Kingdom of God operates exactly opposite to that of the world. Jesus wants you to have all good things in their time, but He wants you to let God give them to you, rather than snatching them for yourself. Hence it is in giving, in surrendering, in "losing" your life that you open your hands to receive it.

By your perseverance you will secure your lives.

-Luke 21:19

Persevere

By standing firm, in patience, in enduring till the end, you will possess your soul. You will keep your life, your eternal life. You will gain the prize. Hold on! Jesus is counting on you.

~ NOVEMBER 13 ~

The people walking in front rebuked him, telling him to be silent, but he kept calling out all the more, "Son of David, have pity on me!"

-Luke 18:39

Son of David!

If you have ever nearly drowned, you know the absolute need to find a way to breathe. In a similar way, blind Bartimaeus will not be satisfied until he gets Jesus' attention. There's a lesson here. God wants you to cry out for Him, with passion and perseverance. He wants your heart to be fully engaged, so hungry for Him. "Have pity on me!"

How many are my foes, LORD!
How many rise against me!
-Psalm 3:2

My Shield

Sometimes your back is against the wall. Enemies enclose you on all sides and you can't see a way out. The verse continues: "But you, LORD, are a shield around me; my glory, you keep my head high" (Psalm 3:3). Today, take up your shield. Use the weapons God is giving you! Go forth to overcome in Him. Amen! Alleluia!

∼ **NOVEMBER 15** ∼

Those whom I love, I reprove and chastise.
Be earnest, therefore, and repent.
-Revelation 3:19

Repent and Return!

There is a certain consolation in this verse. God cares enough about you to not let you go if you're wandering away. He would rather reprove you than coddle you. Be earnest, repent, and return!

"Today salvation has come to this house because this man too is a
descendant of Abraham.
For the Son of Man has come to seek and to save what was lost."
-Luke 19:9-10

Salvation

Today, salvation has come. May this be your day
as well, for the Son of Man came not only to save
Zacchaeus, but you too! Zacchaeus jumped down
from the tree and changed his life. What action will
you take today?

The four living creatures, each of them with six wings, were covered with
eyes inside and out. Day and night they do not stop exclaiming:
"Holy, holy, holy is the Lord God almighty,
who was, and who is, and who is to come."
-Revelation 4:8

Holy, Holy

Just think, while you go about your day, in heaven
a countless throng continually raises a mighty song
to the One seated on the Throne, and to the Lamb.
The amazing truth is, you can join them by praising
God right now. Holy, Holy, Holy!

"'Why did you not put my money in a bank?
Then on my return I would have collected it with interest.'"
-Luke 19:23

Where Is the Interest?

Jesus did not set up His Kingdom immediately on earth. He chose instead to give us giftings that we might join with Him in His eternal enterprise. So... what have you done with the dough? He has given you His authority. How have you used it?

Behold, he is coming amid the clouds,
and every eye will see him,
even those who pierced him
All the peoples of the earth will lament him.
Yes. Amen.
-Revelation 1:7

He Comes Again!

Every person ever created will see Jesus when He returns. And all of us will mourn Him, our Savior, whom we crucified. Imagine that moment. Now, what can you do today to help win for Him the reward of His sufferings?

"Jesus, remember me when you come into your kingdom."

-Luke 23:42

Remember Me

Jesus was in agony when He heard these words. He could have ignored them, but He went outside Himself and used His ebbing strength to offer a deep and saving consolation to the good thief. Today, pray these words with all your heart.

"For whoever does the will of my heavenly Father
is my brother, and sister, and mother."

-Matthew 12:50

Family

Jesus loved His mother Mary more than you can ever know. Yet He does not cling to that, but opens His Heart to you, and shows you how you too can enter that love. Today, what is the will of the Father for you?

"Those others have all made offerings from their surplus wealth,
but she, from her poverty, has offered her whole livelihood."
-Luke 21:4

Everything

It's hard to imagine the selfless generosity and trust of this poor widow. She has truly given her entire living to God. Today, is Jesus also calling you to be a bit more generous? Just say yes!

Giving thanks always and for everything
in the name of our Lord Jesus Christ to God the Father.
-Ephesians 5:20

Thanksgiving

Appreciation is the memory of the heart. The Jews sing a song, "Dayenu" ("It would have been enough"), at Passover. It would have been enough indeed if God had only created us, but He has done so very much more! Today, write down the top ten things for which you are grateful. Dayenu!

Remain faithful until death, and I will give you the crown of life.

-Revelation 2:10

Faithful

Jesus lets us know that some of us will be tested gravely, even unto death. That's not easy to hear. But He adds that He will give us the crown of life. Can you imagine such a scene? Pray today for the strength to be faithful regardless of the death God chooses for you, and for the grace to receive His crown.

Sing a new song to the LORD, who has done marvelous deeds,
Whose right hand and holy arm have won the victory.

-Psalm 98:1

A New Song

God wants us to sing a new song because He's always doing new things—amazing things—in us, around us, and through us. Today, find someone to praise God with, and something new to praise Him for!

"My God has sent his angel and closed the lions' mouths so that they have
not hurt me. For I have been found innocent before him;
neither to you have I done any harm, O king!"
-Daniel 6:22

Delivered!

God has demonstrated continually His power to
save us. Call on Him in any trouble, and He will
deliver you either you from it or through it, to
glorify His Name. What a mighty God we serve!

After this I heard what sounded like the loud voice of a great multitude in
heaven, saying:
"Alleluia!
Salvation, glory, and might belong to our God."
-Revelation 19:1

Alleluia!

There are many who do not accept God's reign, and
do what they can to forestall it. Yet to Him alone
belongs Power, Salvation, glory, and might. You are
wise to trust in Him. Today, add your voice to the
throng in heaven, and sing, "Alleluia! Salvation,
glory, and might belong to our God."

NOVEMBER 28

He received dominion, glory, and kingship;
nations and peoples of every language serve him.
His dominion is an everlasting dominion
that shall not be taken away,
his kingship shall not be destroyed.
-Daniel 7:14

Everlasting Dominion

The Son of Man finally receives His full inheritance. All nations and peoples shall serve Him; His kingship shall not be destroyed. Is is a kingdom of love, of deep, humble, servant love. It is a kingdom of compassion, His compassion, for the weak, the lowly, the little ones of the earth. O Lord, please increase Your kingdom in us! Thank You!

NOVEMBER 29

Heaven and earth will pass away, but my words will not pass away.
-Luke 21:33

The Final Word

The King has spoken. God sent His Word made flesh into the world, not to condemn you, but to save you. Christ has died; Christ is risen. Christ will come again. Amen. Alleluia! Today, let Jesus live in you. Be present to others; share your smile, your heart of His love.

All scripture is inspired by God and is useful for teaching, for refutation, for correction, and for training in righteousness, so that one who belongs to God may be competent, equipped for every good work.

-2 Timothy 3:16-17

All Scripture

God has breathed His presence and power into every word of Scripture, so that it might impart to us spirit and life. Read His Word and receive His Spirit today. Let His Word take root in you. Meditate on it and come alive!

∾ DECEMBER 1 ∾

Come, let us climb the LORD'S mountain,
to the house of the God of Jacob,
That he may instruct us in his ways,
and we may walk in his paths.

-Isaiah 2:3

Return

Today the Church invites you to return to the Lord, to climb His mountain. It is a work, a decision. However, you do not ascend alone, but with your family of Faith. Dear Lord, help me please to hear from You, that You might instruct me and guide me in *Your* ways and in *Your* paths of peace. Amen.

You have been told, O man, what is good, and what the LORD
requires of you: Only to do right and to love goodness,
and to walk humbly with your God.
-Micah 6:8

Act

The Lord calls us to action, deeds that flow from a heart touched by His mercy. His directives are simple and pure: Do right. Love goodness. Walk humbly, with Him. Let us return to our first love, and do as He tells us.

∽ **DECEMBER 3** ∽

"A voice of one crying out in the desert,
'Prepare the way of the Lord,
make straight his paths.'"
-Matthew 3:1-3

Make Straight His Paths

Saint Teresa of Avila wrote, "The reason why so many souls who apply themselves to prayer are not inflamed with God's love is that they neglect to carefully prepare themselves for it." Let us not fail to get our hearts ready for Jesus. Today spend some extra time in prayer. Prepare ye the way!

Be strong, fear not!
Here is your God,
he comes with vindication;
With divine recompense
he comes to save you.
-Isaiah 35:4

Be Not Afraid

God so often tells us, "Be strong, fear not!" because He knows our tendency is just the opposite. Saint Therese of Lisieux taught that the simplest and most direct path to holiness is to abandon yourself completely to God and to entrust yourself to Him as a child relies completely on her father. Today, trust in Him to deliver you!

➣ **DECEMBER 5** ➣

Rise up in splendor! Your light has come,
the glory of the Lord shines upon you.
-Isaiah 60:1

Arise and Shine

God constantly calls us to stand up. He has given you Himself, His Spirit, His salvation, His armor, His Word, and so much more. What are you waiting for? Rise up in splendor, your light has come!

For he rescues the poor when they cry out,
the oppressed who have no one to help.
He shows pity to the needy and the poor
and saves the lives of the poor.
-Psalm 72:12-13

Compassion

Open your heart this Advent. Let justice roll like a river. Feed the homeless, visit the sick, listen to the little ones; be merciful to all. As Mother Teresa said, "Do small things with great love."

"Let us know, let us strive to know the LORD;
as certain as the dawn is his coming,
and his judgment shines forth like the light of day!
He will come to us like the rain,
like spring rain that waters the earth."
·Hosea 6:3

He is Coming!

"God created us without our cooperation," wrote Saint Augustine, "but He will not save us without it." So, am I seeking to know God, to spend time with Him, to obey Him? For just as sure as the sun will arise, He will come, and He will not delay.

"Behold, I am the handmaid of the Lord.
Let it be done unto me according to your word."
-Luke 1:38

Mary

This lovely young lady from Nazareth was a mighty warrior for God! Am I willing to follow her lead and to surrender to God for what He wants to do in me and for what He asks me to do?

For God is leading Israel in joy
by the light of his glory,
with his mercy and justice for company.
-Baruch 5:9

Not Alone

It is God who always takes the initiative with you, even when you do not realize it. He will keep all of His promises to you, regardless of how long it may take. His work in your life is bright, for He leads you by the brilliant light of His glory, with tender compassion and lovingkindness.

This is my prayer: that your love may increase ever more and more in knowledge and every kind of perception, to discern what is of value, so that you may be pure and blameless for the day of Christ.

-Philippians 1:9-10

Increase

Are you growing in the love of Christ? Saint Paul prays that you may increase in the grace that stimulates you to do good for others, to reach out and touch, to serve with humility. In so doing, you will come to know what's really important, what is God's perfect will, and you will come to be pure and without blame on the last day.

∽ **DECEMBER 11** ∽

He gives strength to the fainting;
for the weak he makes vigor abound.

-Isaiah 40:29

My Strength

God delights in renewing us. He wants to save us. We may feel we're done in, but He's never done delivering us! Wait on the Lord, and ask for His help. "The name of the LORD is a strong tower; the just man runs to it and is safe" (Proverbs 18:10).

‿‿ DECEMBER 12 ‿‿

And Mary said:

"My soul proclaims the greatness of the Lord."

-Luke 1:46

Magnificat

Let us, with Mary, rejoice in the Lord in our spirits, and magnify Him in our hearts this Advent. In fact, ask Mary to teach you how to rejoice in the Lord always, to magnify Him more today than you did yesterday. She is the Queen!

‿‿ DECEMBER 13 ‿‿

He was not the light, but came to testify to the light.

-John 1:8

Testify to the Light

We are called to humility on one hand, for only Jesus is *the* Light; yet to boldness on the other, for He desires that we let Him shine His light in us! Today, tell someone what God has done for you or through you, even if it is something small. Ask Jesus to light up another's life through you.

ᵔᵕᵔ DECEMBER 14 ᵔᵕᵔ

Rejoice in the Lord always. I shall say it again: rejoice!
-Philippians 4:4

Rejoice!

To be joyful in the Lord is to demonstrate our childlike trust in Him. It is to proclaim to the world that, regardless of how things may appear, our God reigns! As Saint Teresa of Avila said, "May God protect us from sad saints."

ᵔᵕᵔ DECEMBER 15 ᵔᵕᵔ

He said to them in reply, "Whoever has two cloaks should share with the person who has none. And whoever has food should do likewise."
-Luke 3:11

Share and Care

The Church has always taught that the person who withholds charity is stealing from the poor, since the goods of the earth belong to all the people of the earth. Reflect today on the Sea of Galilee, which flows out into the Jordan River, and remains fresh and vital. The Dead Sea, on the other hand, keeps all its water, and is a salty waste.

A star shall advance from Jacob,
and a staff shall rise from Israel.
-Numbers 24:17

A Star Shall Rise

God's ways are not our ways. He sees far ahead and works now to prepare the fulfillment of His promises. And His promises are out of this world! Read the promises of God in His Word. Let them build up faith within you, for "faith comes from what is heard, and what is heard comes through the word of Christ" (Romans 10:17).

~~ **DECEMBER 17** ~~

"Amen, I say to you, tax collectors and prostitutes
are entering the kingdom of God before you."
-Matthew 21:31

Tax Collectors and Prostitutes

The Shepherd cares for all His sheep, especially those who lose their way. When the "sinners" of Jesus' day heard John the Baptist, they repented. Today, join Jesus in His search by being open to everyone you meet, and loving them with *His* heart.

Turn to me and be safe,
all you ends of the earth,
for I am God; there is no other!
-Isaiah 45:22

Return to Me

Many voices promise us endless possibilities, but only God has a track record of always delivering. Today, turn to Him. Abandon yourself to Him. Renew your trust in Your Father and in His Son, the Savior. Ask God to hold you in His arms and embrace you to His bosom. Love Him; He loves you.

◦◦◦ DECEMBER 19 ◦◦◦

God, you have taught me from my youth;
to this day I proclaim your wondrous deeds.
-Psalm 71:17

Faithful

God is faithful, the God who has helped you, guided you, accompanied you, forgiven you, loved you, surrounded you with family and friends, and has blessed you since your youth and even before your birth! Today, tell somebody one thing that God has done for you!

"He will rule over the house of Jacob forever,

and of his kingdom there will be no end."

-Luke 1:33

Forever

As a child, Saint Teresa of Avila was so impressed by spiritual things that she would sometimes exclaim, "O Eternity! O Eternity! To be tormented during a whole eternity! To rejoice during a whole eternity! To be without end in pain! To be without end in joy! Who can find words for it?" Indeed. Today, continue to progress in the way of perfection, one step at a time. Of *His* Kingdom, there will be no end.

∽ DECEMBER 21 ∽

The LORD, your God, is in your midst,

a mighty savior;

He will rejoice over you with gladness,

and renew you in his love.

-Zephaniah 3:17

Made New

Are you feeling used up? God has promised to renew you, to make you new in His love. He will send forth His Spirit, and renew His creation ... even now. He will rejoice! And so will you!

Lift up your heads, O gates;
rise up, you ancient portals
that the king of glory may enter.
-Psalm 24:7

Lift Them Up!

God always prepares the way before He moves.
Hence the Psalmist is calling on the gates of the
Holy City to open up before His King. It is time
for you also to lift up your heart so that the King of
glory may enter *you!*

∽ **DECEMBER 23** ∽

Lo, I will send you
Elijah, the prophet,
Before the day of the LORD comes,
the great and terrible day,
To turn the hearts of the fathers to their children,
and the hearts of the children to their fathers.
-Malachi 23:24

Fathers and Children

In His mercy, the Lord promises to fill the hearts of
parents and children with renewed affection, that
we might all be ready for the King of Love. Today,
ask Him to forgive you of any resentment and to fill
you with tenderness for the members of your family.

*"Behold, I stand at the door and knock. If anyone hears my voice and opens
the door, [then] I will enter his house and dine with him, and he with me."*
-Revelation 3:20

Listen!

Joseph and Mary search for welcome as twilight
descends upon the little town of Bethlehem. Yet all
doors are closed. How about in your heart? Do you
hear the gentle yet persistent knock? Are you home?
If so, will you open the door? Remember, they will
look just like any other homeless couple.

∽ **DECEMBER 25** ∽

For a child is born to us, a son is given us;
upon his shoulder dominion rests.
They name him Wonder-Counselor, God-Hero,
Father-Forever, Prince of Peace.
-Isaiah 9:5

A Son

In the midnight skies surrounding a dusty stable,
the Sun of Righteousness, the Son of God, is born,
more human than any of us, divine warrior come
in helpless disguise to rescue His own. Behold your
King!

The people who walked in darkness
have seen a great light;
Upon those who dwelt in the land of gloom
a light has shone.
-Isaiah 9:1

A Great Light

Only those in darkness can truly appreciate the light. Brilliant rays emanate from the heart of the newborn Babe, which will one day renew all creation. A light *has* shone! Now, call upon God to fill you with this light. As Pope Francis has said, "We are not living an era of change, but a change of era." Only Jesus can usher in true and eternal righteousness.

Put on then, as God's chosen ones, holy and beloved, heartfelt compassion,
kindness, humility, gentleness, and patience.
-Colossians 3:12

Put on Christ!

Do not try to work up virtue by your own power, but put on the garment of goodness that God Himself provides, in simplicity and trust. Only He can give you heartfelt tenderness and humble patience. Let the Christ Child love through you as you continue to celebrate this holy season. 189

"Out of Egypt I called my son."
-Matthew 2:15

Come out!

God has called you out of your past, your slavery to sin, into a new life. Are you walking with Him or are you wandering in the desert? Today, choose life! Consider joining others in your battle against sin and pernicious habits that would keep you from entering and taking possession of the Promised Land.

*And yet I do write a new commandment to you, which holds true in him
and among you, for the darkness is passing away,
and the true light is already shining.*
-1 John 2:8

A New Commandment

How can you participate in this awesome light which has come to earth? Let Jesus love through you. It's that simple, if you let it be. As Saint John of the Cross said, "In the evening of life, we will be judged on love alone."

Whoever loves his brother remains in the light,
and there is nothing in him to cause a fall.
-1 John 2:10

Remain in the Light

Jesus seeks faith and works, love and goodness. To act in love is to remain in the stream of God's light, and it can only bring good. Ask God daily for the grace to love others, and then look for ways to show it in word and deed.

The one who gives this testimony says, "Yes, I am coming soon." Amen!
Come, Lord Jesus!
The grace of the Lord Jesus be with all.
-Revelation 22:20-21

Amen.

God is merciful; there is a time for the fulfillment of all righteousness. A final, definitive moment will arrive, when Jesus returns to judge the world and set up His Kingdom. Jesus gives us His word: "I am coming soon." Even so, Lord Jesus, come! Amen.

A Final Word

No one has ever seen God.
The only Son, God, who is at the Father's side, has revealed him.

-John 1:18

We are engaged in a great battle, a conflict that has raged ever since the Garden of Eden. We were created for fellowship with God, to be stewards and rulers of His awesome creation. But we turned away from God, deceived by the enemy into doubting His Word and His love for us.

The good news, the astoundingly wonderful news, is that God did not turn away from us. In His divine mercy He promised us a Redeemer. He then began to woo us back to Himself, one heart at a time. It can take a long time to move a heart by love versus force, but God is patient.

And so God's own Word, which was with Him from the beginning, and which is Himself God, became flesh and dwelled among us. Jesus, the Son of God, delivered us God's message in person, and He has given us life—eternal, abundant, overflowing life. May you continue to receive His Word daily into your hearts, and may you truly come alive in Him. Amen. Alleluia!